Reflections From Another Side

Mental Illness Survivors and Advocates

Unite to Write

I0223970

Anthology

by Residents and Staff of Royal Ottawa Place

Directed and Collated by Chris Nihmey

chipmunkapublishing
the mental health publisher

Published by
Chipmunkapublishing
United Kingdom

http://www.chipmunkapublishing.co.uk

Copyright © 2018 Chris Nihmey

ISBN   978-1-78382-370-3

Special thanks to Mario Jamora, illustrator for front/back covers ... beautiful!

Another special thank you from all resident writers and caregivers to The Royal (Royal Ottawa Mental Health Centre) and ROP (Royal Ottawa Place) for their continued support with this initiative. Mary Baskin and Beverly Cummings ... your assistance with editing was invaluable. We cannot thank you enough.

For all without a place to call home

ACKNOWLEDGEMENTS

With acceptance and compassion, the possibilities are endless.

Thank you, God, and everyone who contributed to making this special book a reality. Thanks to you, Dad, for your wisdom, your guidance, and your continued support. Thank you, Mom, for being a beacon of hope in my life. I now share your message with others. See you one day soon. Make sure the coffee is on. The stone has been tossed; the first ripple has formed. Hope begins.

TABLE OF CONTENTS

June 10, 2017

Dear Diary,

It was another one of those days. I can't stand it. I don't know what to do anymore. It's awful. Terrible. Work sucks. School sucks. I never want to go back. Kids suck! He's going to hurt me. His friends will, too. I hate the names, I hate the rumours, I hate them! My parents aren't even paying attention to me. It's like I'm not even there. I feel so alone, by myself. Maybe I want to be alone. Maybe? Maybe not.

The thoughts are back again, the feelings are where they were a month ago. My head feels heavy, I just don't know which way to turn. I can't stop these thoughts, these actions. I can't get rid of these awful feelings. I just want to throw my medication away. It doesn't even feel like it's doing a damn thing! I hate my life! What is wrong with me? I look in the mirror and I can't stand looking at myself. I'm ugly. I'm worthless. I really don't know if I'm going to get through this. I don't know if I'm going to make it through another day … Anne

INTRODUCTION

Chris Nihmey

It would take me a long time to achieve "IT ALL", but I learned the hard way: that you can LOSE everything. That doesn't take long at all.

In 2001, my world came crashing down. In just four words from my doctor, my life was torn apart. "You have bipolar disorder." With these four words, I knew my life was about to change forever, and not for the better. I would no longer be what people termed "normal". I would now carry a label that I would bear for life ... a scab, a scar. I swore a vow of silence that day, that my disorder would remain a secret. I would carry the load all by myself. I would not tell anyone. I could not tell anyone. How dare I? What was I now?

I chose not to be labelled a sicko, a psycho, less than…. I would embark on a journey that would inch on, day after day, moment by moment, for well over a decade. My family and I, the four of us, would choose to conceal, to protect, to hide a secret so profound that, if revealed, could literally destroy every part of me. I would "live a lie" to shield myself from harsh prejudice and judgement. Never would they know. Never would I face the thoughts and actions of a society which, most often, lacks compassion and acceptance for those who carry this disease: invisible ... one that cannot be seen, but, for some reason, is judged so readily. "I'm fine" became my motto. I wore a mask to protect myself. I thought I'd wear it forever.

It would be a challenge, the toughest of its kind. Although my illness was "invisible", I would learn quickly that the consequences of the disorder were clearly visible, leaving damaging effects on my life. I would also learn about unfortunate souls, afflicted and wounded, who dared to step into the light, to reveal their truth, hoping to be accepted. They would then be scorned by society. Courageous? More like a sentence! I would not let it happen to me.

Afflicted by a sickness that others cannot fully comprehend, what can one do? The answer is simple: you don't! Many people choose not to try to comprehend or understand mental illness. "They" find it easier to mistreat, to bully, to belittle, to disrespect, and to hurt someone they don't fully understand. Does it make them feel better, bigger? Is it fear? I call it ignorance, injustice, and intolerance. Mental illness is like an illusion. People choose to see what they want to see. Ignorance develops into fear, which can foster hate. When these lead the way, the victim is either bullied or has to hide. Silence is the result. Our kids are hurting. More and more, our youth are afraid to talk, until it's too late. We can't let the loss of a loved one's life be their call for help. The sufferer has nothing left to hang onto, no one to reach for. Fear then wins.

We can make a decision to stop the silence. No one should be alone. Alone leads to drastic measures; ending one's life is never a choice. No one in their "right" healthy mind would choose to die. Sickness makes this choice, as does abuse, bullying, addiction, rejection, and isolation. How we treat someone IS a choice. We should be saying to them, "It should not end this way. I'm here." Talking saves lives. We need to open up avenues for sufferers to speak up and reach for help early. When we do this, hope and healing begin, and the road to recovery is not as treacherous, and is less daunting.

"In the end, we will remember not the words of our enemies, but the silence of our friends."

Martin Luther King Jr.

Dr. King's words call out to each of us to change. He is telling us that, in silence, we all suffer. We must speak the truth and stand up for what is right. Otherwise, we end up living in a society lacking compassion and acceptance. We, the sick, become invisible.

I hid. I lied. I saved my life. No one would know about the three severe disorders I carried. My loving family would support me unconditionally. They are the reason I'm alive today. Stereotypes, false myths, and stigma hurt. They debilitate a sufferer. But what if you cannot hide? What if coming clean is something you cannot control? There are warriors, both men and women, exposed, abused, and most times rejected for the patch they wear: many kicked out of their homes because of their ailments, ending up living on a friend's basement couch. From there, thrown into a system that didn't, or couldn't, offer the proper support needed, there was nowhere else to turn. There was never an opportunity to hide, to conceal, to form a lie. When push came to shove, they were alone. From the couch, they would turn to their saviours: the bottle, the puff, the needle. Damaged goods. These would destroy a beautiful mind that, at one time, had the potential to thrive and flourish. Self-medicating often results. However, this will point a sufferer in the opposite direction of healing, as they abuse substances that prohibit healing. Had I resorted to substances like marijuana in my quest to heal, I would still be stuck in my parents' dark basement, a hole in which I dwelled during my major depression in 2001. Doctor-ordered prescription medication was a crucial part of my healing, and it helped save my life. Self-medicating with a substance like marijuana would have destroyed me. It is damaging, it is a depressant, it kills our brain, and is especially dangerous for our youth, and those suffering from mental illness. Studies have shown that there is an increased risk of the symptoms of psychosis among youth users and, in some, schizophrenia is triggered, a lifelong mental illness, one of the most difficult to live with. Under 25, over 25, it doesn't matter; marijuana, or any street drug, will prevent healing. Our lives matter. A sufferer often feels that their life does not matter.

Without support, without love, these sufferers would fall victim to addiction, which, in turn, would point them in a hazardous direction. The streets would become their kingdom, their shelter, their bandage. However, in this kingdom, there is no knight to come to their aid. There is only their fellow victim: incapable, disregarded, and lost. They would lose confidence and self-esteem rapidly. Many would be left to die, physically or mentally, without any other option. Some would be committed to a life behind prison walls, while others would die, victims of self-abuse. Many, unfortunately, would take their own lives to end the pain. Sickness would win.

Where there's a will, they say, there's a way. Some might call it chance. I prefer "things happening for a reason". Among the many unfortunate souls who suffered, who fought the battle lines of rejection, impoverishment, and mental abuse, some made it out of this dark abyss alive, weathering the storm. They managed to find the appropriate help: therapy, medication, and a support system. They would begin to form a new society, realizing that they are not alone, and that maybe, maybe they do matter.

Broken down and mentally exhausted, they would walk, or crawl, to feel this liveliness, this acceptance. For the first time in their lives, they would feel something greater. They were alive and would live to see another day. They would become a select group of men and women who would become "survivors".

I took my own path, blessed with my wonderful family and trusted doctor, who would not give up on me, despite my ill-chosen actions. With these supports, and hard work on my part, I, too, became one of them: a survivor. It would be an excruciating journey. Day after day, month after month, I would fight to stay alive. Surrounded by those who cared for me, I would continue to struggle, falling time and time again, but I would not give up. Regardless of the pain, regardless of the suffering, I would move on quietly, silently, my story untold. Solitude would be my saving grace. "They" would not find out. I would not be labelled. I would not be frowned upon. I would march on: a survivor. Regardless of feeling alone within, I would find the way to live on, to breathe, and to find some kind of hope: to search and find better days.

Each of us would search for hope and healing in our own ways and, like all survivors, we would fight with the ultimate intent of one day becoming … "visible". To finally matter. To realize that we have a voice, and that our illness is not our fault. To be able to finally remove the mask we once donned, and be accepted for who we are.

Whether we hide to avoid stigma or discrimination, or whether we are forced to share our stories due to circumstances beyond our control, no one wants to be labelled invisible. Regardless of the mental illness we carry, we do matter, much like someone who has cancer, heart disease, or diabetes. Pain is pain: body or brain. They are all illnesses, disorders, diseases, however we choose to label them. The difference lies in the acceptance of, and compassion for, those who suffer. Until mental illness sufferers are viewed in a different light, much like cancer victims who receive immediate sympathy, mental illness sufferers will continue to remain invisible. My dear mother, my hero, passed away from cancer in 2014. After the battle she endured, I've met no greater a champion. But there are so many other sufferers who deserve similar accolades. I've met them. I've battled alongside them. Though measures are being implemented in our schools and organizations to destigmatize and decrease intolerance and indifference, we, as a society, have to work harder. The road is still *less travelled*. (Robert Frost)

"Four-eyes, dummy, incapable, retarded, cripple, loser, weak, irresponsible, freak, slow, mentally-challenged, pitiful, less than, alone. Change is necessary."

ROP Resident

OUR INSPIRATION

In 2009, I began volunteering with several residents at Royal Ottawa Place (ROP), an affiliate of the Royal Ottawa Mental Health Centre, one of the leading mental health centres in Canada. ROP is a long-term care home that houses men and women with severe mental and physical disabilities, the majority lacking outside support or care. Some come from hospitals, others are victims of stigma, rejected by family and friends, and others, from the streets.

On my second visit to the home, I met a special girl, Nathalie, and she touched me forever. It happened for a reason. Nathalie suffered from a rare hereditary illness, Huntington's disease. She was only in her early thirties when I met her. Huntington's disease is like living in a prison cell that is the size of your body. I walked into her room and was hit with the shock of a lifetime. There she lay on her back, helpless, shaking uncontrollably, every muscle twitching, sweating profusely, as she grunted and groaned, staring at the ceiling. As thin as a rake, her eyes half-rolled, she could barely speak. She could not eat on her own. Her legs constantly kicked the bed rails that protected her from falling out. She had thick padding around her legs to prevent bruising. I had never seen anything as terrible as this. Who knew at the time, that it would be a life-changing moment for Nathalie? It would also be a life-changing moment for me.

Over the next year or so, I worked on improving communication with her, hoping to understand her needs better. I devised a homemade picture board to help her with speech and communication. It was a struggle for her, but when we found success, we both celebrated. These were moments I would not forget, along with many walks in her wheelchair, and special occasions together.

In January of 2011, Nathalie became ill with a high fever. Since her body was constantly moving, her core temperature could not be brought down. She entered the hospital and, in only a week, sadly, Nathalie passed away. It would be the last we'd see her. Her loss deeply saddened me. I knew it could not end here.

It did not. Nathalie left us, heading for a place of peace and serenity, but she left behind a gift: inspiration. She left me with a creative idea, a "must do". She left me with a vision, a way that I could reach out to every person who suffers as she did, whether mental or physical. She pointed me in the direction of an idea that would change the face of mental illness, and our perception of those who suffer, including myself. A few weeks after her passing, I brought a pad and pen to the residence and began a journey that would last close to three years. Much like my time with Nathalie, I began to work, to communicate one-on-one with residents at ROP, putting together their thoughts, their emotions, their dreams, and their struggles. Their words and their ideas began to flow and I was astounded! Their eyes lit up every time I walked into their room. Healing, enlightenment, purpose, and meaning, would begin to form.

How could they write and think like this? I finally came to the realization that these beautiful people were definitely trapped within a society that would not foster their creative thinking. Inside the home, they were accepted, treated with compassion and love. But outside, they were seen as sick, menacing, and a hindrance, all because of their illnesses. This was going to change. It just had to. Word by word, writing began to transform our lives, one page at a time.

Nathalie is dear to my heart, and a story that I wrote about her impact on my life can be found at the end of this anthology. This story is about a true champion and this entry is Nathalie's contribution to our book.

OUR PURPOSE

It was my mother who urged me to start volunteering in 2009, when I was yearning to find a deeper sense of hope and healing in my life. She said it would be therapeutic; in giving, I would find healing. I disagreed. Sickness left me feeling so negative about myself. Though I kept my secret hidden, self-stigma told me, time and time again, that I was worthless and going nowhere. So much was taken from me. Thank God, Mom had another vision which, at that time, I could not see. Eventually, I would. It was with apathy and much apprehension that I walked into ROP.

I met men and women who shared a similar passion: a yearning to heal, to find hope, and to be able to reach out. We each suffered in our own way. We were living through the pain and suffering from disorders that took over every part of our minds, bodies, and souls. We had to face the harsh brutality of a society that most often saw us as incapable. In my eyes, we are far from this. No longer should we be labelled invisible. We are survivors.

Having gone through hell and back in my own journey, through years of intensive therapy, with diligence in taking prescribed medication, and a multitude of life changes, I now march to a different tune. I use writing to reach out, to change mindsets, to challenge, and to develop the capacity to love and respect one another. It doesn't matter what faith you follow; we all agree with these same principles.

Writing is therapeutic. It is healing, and it is life. It certainly saved my life. Writing my own memoir, **Two Sides To The Story: Living A Lie**, gave me purpose and meaning beyond my suffering. To be able to write is to be able to share your message of hope and encouragement. We can make a difference, no matter what struggles we endure. I believe we have a duty to share our triumphs and successes with others, to show them that healing does happen. Healing is exponential. It gathers momentum, further and faster. It all begins with one small step. I have healed substantially and continue to take steps forward each day. If I don't share my story, what good was anything I went through? Don't we all have a story we can share that would reach out to someone and make a difference?

You are about to meet 11 mental health advocates (myself included), along with 15 survivors (myself included) who are still fighting their day-to-day battles, and have realized the power of words. Words can destroy; but even more, they can build resilience, strength, and confidence, a "never give up" attitude that is contagious. We can make a difference within and beyond. These many amazing individuals have joined my ensemble, each with their own tune and beat. We are equipping ourselves with the tools to stand strong and be victorious. To stay healthy, we need to be disciplined and responsible. Battling illness is a full-time job. We must realize that, regardless of our circumstances, we can better ourselves and the world. We must continue to reach for better days, and realize that "we" are the key to bettering our lives.

We have survived for a reason. We are now speaking up. We speak for those who can't. Suffering is not a waste of time. It is a stepping stone toward greater things. It is time to open our eyes to what matters. Please read, hear, be educated, and inspired, through our words of faith, hope, purpose, healing, and love.

Our anthology, appropriately titled **Reflections From Another Side**, has not only become a sharing of talents but, equally, has become a strong force in the fight against the terrible stigma that surrounds mental illness. What these writers have accomplished is remarkable. Mental illness should not hold us back. It cannot keep a person from living a quality life, from sharing, and from being an example of faith, hope, integrity, strength and courage. These residents have proven to me that, no matter what we face in life, we can survive. It is not what we earn in life that makes the difference, it is what we overcome. Booker T. Washington, a civil rights leader and advisor to presidents of the United States in the early 1900s, stated that *success should be measured by the many obstacles we overcome, even more so than the position we have reached.* These men and women have proven that we can accomplish anything we put our minds to. We have all taken great leaps. We need to celebrate these victories if society is going to change its views. Healing is, by far, the greatest thing I have ever accomplished. In suffering, we do find purpose and meaning in our lives.

I directed, mentored, and collaborated with each resident writer to produce his or her own individual work(s). I worked diligently to guide them to produce a short story, a type of poem, a type of procedural work, a letter, a biography, or an autobiography. I took each resident through the writing process from an "idea" to a "ready to be published" piece of work. I used brainstorming charts and planning sheets to help them with the process. These can be found at the end of this book. My teaching experience was definitely an asset in the writing process. Each, despite their obstacles, has contributed a wonderful piece of writing. With some guidance and direction, I have been amazed with what we've produced. This book is evidence that sufferers can accomplish great things of beauty and creativity when they feel supported, accepted and loved. Our goal now is to join in the fight against stigma, with the ultimate goal of eradicating it forever. If I had stigmatized these individuals, this would not have happened. Nothing would have happened, except hurt and pain. Instead, by being vulnerable, and sharing the true essence of who they are, these men and women have found purpose and meaning beyond their suffering and, because of this, their hidden talents emerged. I saw beyond the illness, and lives changed considerably, including my own.

These writers have overcome profound obstacles in their lives that most of us could not even comprehend. Regardless of their illnesses, each has produced an incredible piece of writing. A handful of entries were written solely by the resident. We worked together to shape, edit, and revise their story to get it ready for publishing. It was very rewarding for them.

It is time to stop using the words, "they can't", and start using "they can". Useless, disregarded, incapable ... NO. Useful, highly regarded, and capable. This book was written to inspire. It is a call to all of us to reach for change, to act, and to stand united together.

"Lean on me, when you're not strong. And I'll be your friend. I'll help you carry on."

Lean On me, 1972
Bill Withers

YOU HAVE CHANGED OUR LIVES

ROYAL OTTAWA PLACE CAREGIVERS

Debbie Pilon

Manager of Resident and Family Services and Recreation Therapy

I was very excited to see this project become a book. I have had the pleasure of working at Royal Ottawa Place since it opened, and it is a very special place. The residents involved in this project are excited and proud of their writings. It is an honour for them to be able to share their words with the world. Thank you, Chris, for giving them this opportunity to express themselves and share their talents. Congratulations to all the resident writers involved in this project.

Erin Langiano

Recreation Therapist

I am very fortunate to be a Recreation Therapist at Royal Ottawa Place. I started in 2004, as a volunteer. Officially, I became a permanent employee in 2005. I have been working at ROP for many years now, which is hard to believe. Time really does fly here, because we have so much fun.

As a Recreation Therapist, I wear many hats on a day-to-day basis. My main role is to ensure that each resident has a meaningful leisure lifestyle, individually, and in both small and large group activities. Community integration and independent leisure are vital for our residents. In our department, we feel that it is important to have strong community connections, and ensure that each resident feels part of their community. Some of my favourite community programs are: the Terry Fox Run (raising over $2,000), the Wiggle Waggle Walkathon (raising $500), boat trips with friends, sports fishing, and propeller dance.

Over the last many years of working at ROP, I have had the opportunity to work with approximately 209 residents. I have seen residents return to their homes in the community, reach their goals, decline, pass away, move to be closer to their loved ones, or move due to the closure of our first floor. Most of all, I have seen so many residents at ROP live healthy lifestyles: mentally, physically, spiritually, emotionally, and socially.

ROP is like a big family. Many of our residents have lived there since we opened the doors in 2004. They listen to, and support one another on a daily basis. They look out for one another, fight like sisters or brothers might, and are aware of one another's daily schedules. Some see their family members. For the many who don't, they are blessed to see many staff, volunteers, and students coming in and out. They look forward to these interactions. Not only are the residents amazing to work with, I have had the pleasure of working with terrific volunteers, students, and staff who, as a team, have worked to enhance the residents' well-being. I feel very privileged to know that I am making a difference in the lives of our residents.

I am inspired by the residents I work with. Nothing beats the feeling of watching a resident try a new leisure activity and enjoy it, or having residents reach goals we set for them. Since working here, I have seen so many of our residents improving. Many people who have a mental illness don't take care of a lot of the basics and, therefore, have a hard time enjoying leisure. We work on this daily. We work with the residents to take care of these basics, such as proper sleep, eating balanced meals, taking medications, having friendships in a secure environment, and reconnecting with family members they may not have seen for years.

Over the years, I have shared so many of my own personal life experiences with the residents. I've married, travelled, and was able to share pictures of these life-changing events during our armchair travel programs. I now have two beautiful babies as well. Every day I come in to work, the residents ask me about my family. I ask them about their lives. These are critical interactions that open up their lives. It is these small interactions that make a difference in the residents' lives, and also in mine.

A special memory at ROP is difficult for me to find. Every day at ROP is very special. Every day is not easy and, like everyone in the world, I have difficult days as well. But when it comes down to it, I don't look at working at ROP as just a job. It is something much grander. Working at ROP makes my life complete.

Amy Leroy

Recreation Therapist

Royal Ottawa Place is more than just a long-term care residence on the grounds of the Royal Ottawa Mental Health Centre. It is also a home for many wonderful individuals I have had the privilege of working with, who have become very special people in my life. I was a recreation therapy student a number of years ago, and my internship supervisor suggested that I apply for a student placement at ROP. Little did I know at the time, but I was walking through the doors of a building that would change my life in so many ways.

As a Recreation Therapist, I play many roles on the team at ROP. I provide the residents with opportunities to pursue their recreation and leisure interests, either on their own, or in a structured group program. A lot of "behind-the-scenes" work goes on in our office, whether we are planning our Christmas celebrations, doing accounting spreadsheets, or supervising students and volunteers. My job requires a lot of energy, and much creativity, patience, and flexibility. I often share my own talents and interests with the residents, such as my love of music and guitar playing. We have our "ups and downs" days, but every day is unique. We are always aiming to make a difference in the lives of our residents, and the lives of those they impact in the community: for example, the carwash we held to raise money to help find a cure for Huntington's disease.

I could talk forever about all of the wonderful experiences I have had so far at ROP. It is a great community and each resident has taken an entirely different path in life. I love getting to know them. Each carries his or her own story. My job allows me many opportunities to spend positive time with residents, and to be able to lead them through activities and experiences that are meaningful to them. It is a thrill for me to load up our van with the residents and head off on our adventures. Some of my favourite outings have been trips to various beaches, fishing trips and, especially, a wonderful day when I brought some residents to my parents' dairy cattle and horse farm. What an experience! My dad had a tractor and wagon ready for us, equipped with a set of stairs to climb with ease. We went on a fun hayride, enjoyed a lunch made by my mom, and visited with our friendly horses. I made a slideshow of pictures following the visit and shared it with residents who could not be there. That day was magical. We never thought it could be done. Anything is possible at ROP. I have dealt with my fair share of challenges over the years. I work very closely with the residents and have developed bonds with many of them. I often use music as a way of helping residents deal with difficult times. As a student, I paired up with a resident who had many inner struggles. My way of helping him cope was through music. Even on his darkest days, after I played a few strums on my guitar, he would start singing. I will never forget how surprised I was to hear his deep, heartfelt voice. I still get chills thinking about it. We became quite the duo. Those were very special moments for both of us. I could always use music to create a more positive atmosphere, which helped him cooperate with other staff at the home. He would still complain, of course, but I wouldn't let him give up. I even encouraged him to come on a fishing trip with me. We created a beautiful bond and, when he became ill, I visited him at the hospital several times. The last time I went to see him, he was blowing me kisses. Though I tried to deny it, he knew it would be the last time we'd see each other. It was a difficult time for me when he passed on, but I will always cherish the memories I have of him. We deeply impacted each other.

Being a Recreation Therapist at ROP is so much more than a job. It is my life and we make a difference every day. It is a rewarding place to be involved, and the residents have become family. I hope to continue to be a part of their daily lives, sing many more songs with them, and celebrate their success over the years to come.

Janine Bakelaar

Recreation Therapist

In 2013, I had the privilege of spending an entire year working with some of the most inspirational individuals I have ever met, as a Recreation Therapist at Royal Ottawa Place.

I graduated from the University of Waterloo with a degree in Therapeutic Recreation and Leisure Studies, with Honours in Fine Arts. ROP was my first position in the "real world" and I couldn't have been more excited to begin!

I was extremely nervous my first day. However, I learned quickly that there was nothing to be nervous about. I was warmly welcomed by all the residents, staff, and volunteers at ROP. I quickly learned how to be flexible when it came to planning programs. I never could have predicted or imagined how much I would eventually learn from all of the residents who participated.

Some of my favourite memories are of taking residents into the community. Whether it was a designated para-outing, or a trip in the big blue van, there was always an adventure to be had. In the community, I really got to learn more about our residents and took time to enjoy their presence. It always brought a smile to my face to see the joy on the residents' faces when they had the opportunity to enjoy a moment that was out of the ordinary.

There were always exciting things going on at ROP as well. Having the opportunity to help plan and assist with these events was a blast. From ROP's country week, to talent show, to Christmas choir tour, to endless birthday parties and bingo games, there was always something wonderful going on.

Although the halls were often filled with laughter and excitement, there were obviously many hardships, frustrations, and emotionally difficult situations. These reminded me that life can be pretty difficult at times. I spent a lot of time with residents who were at risk of isolation, and who required a lot of encouragement, motivation, and support to help them be part of the community at ROP. I witnessed how important it is for individuals to be given a voice, to be listened to, and to be motivated to make positive decisions in their lives. Witnessing residents coming on outings or attending programs, who before chose to remain in their rooms, demonstrated to me how the healing process takes place. I feel so blessed to have been in a position where I had the opportunity to witness progress and improvements in residents' lives through the use of meaningful recreation.

The life lessons I gained through the residents of ROP will forever impact me as I continue the journey forward in my own life. Their talents and abilities were like nothing I ever expected. ROP is most definitely a true testimony of how the stigma of mental health needs to be eliminated. Sufferers are capable of great things when they are accepted and feel they can succeed.

Working with residents at ROP has inspired me to live each moment to the fullest. Everything you know can be drastically changed forever. I am very thankful for the opportunity I had to meet so many wonderful people. I will forever be impacted by their generosity, their happiness, and their hope for better days ahead.

Kellie Halligan

Recreation Therapist

I've been working as a Recreation Therapist at Royal Ottawa Place for nearly two years now, and it has been such a wonderful experience. There are some truly great people who live there that I have had the pleasure of working with and getting to know. As a Recreation Therapist, I help to plan leisure activities that are geared at achieving goals and promoting health and well-being. I get to interact with the residents on a daily basis and have gotten to know their strengths. I see them reaching goals, forming strong connections, telling jokes, laughing, making difficult decisions, and helping their friends, family, and community. It has been a great opportunity! Sitting down to write about a single moment was so difficult, because one just led to another, and another, and so on … which eventually just led to lots of smiling! As a Recreation Therapist, I get to see them enjoying life. They have good days and bad days. While they face stigma and adversities, many continue to show drive and motivation each day. They are an inspiring group of people and it has been a pleasure getting to know each of them.

Jessica Stewart

Recreation Therapist

In the summer of 2013, I had the privilege of working with ROP residents while completing a four-month internship for my post-graduate education in Recreation Therapy. During my internship, I was given the opportunity to work with each resident, designing and implementing recreation programs that encouraged their independence, as well as focusing on their individual interests and strengths. I provided the residents with emotional, social, physical, and intellectual stimulation through a variety of recreation programs, such as music-based programs, barbecues, birthday parties, fitness programs, outings, luncheons and, of course, bingo!

I chose to do my internship at ROP because I love people. I really enjoyed hearing their stories, talking to them about where they'd come from, and getting to know and understand them as individuals. I came to respect and admire them for who they are. The work that I do is not only my job, it is my passion. The residents at ROP may have severe and persistent mental and physical health issues, but what I saw were people with likes, dislikes, interests, talents, and passions of their own. I always wanted to find out who the person is on the inside. Many of the residents at ROP have amazing spirits and wonderful positive outlooks on life. They have inspired me to see past everyday struggles and hardships, and to stay optimistic and hopeful no matter what challenges I face.

Self-stigma is a constant and daily obstacle that residents face due to their illnesses. Sue Racine, a resident and fellow writer at ROP, who has become a good friend of mine, lives with this stigma every day. She understands her illnesses, and has therefore blamed and even resented her ailments. It is upsetting to see how much she believes her disability affects her happiness in life. I do understand her sadness. She has watched family and friends around her experience those milestone events, like finding a partner, getting married, and starting a family. Although her illnesses have prevented her from accomplishing some of these things, she realizes that these are not the quintessential elements to obtaining a fulfilling and satisfying life. By educating herself and learning about her illnesses, she has been able to look past her problems and focus on finding solutions. Although she still struggles, receiving support and encouragement helps her to build confidence. This allows her to remain as strong and independent as possible. Finding meaningful activities and a role within ROP has increased her self-confidence and decreased the self-stigma she sometimes experiences. These attempts to reduce self-stigma are a big part of what we, as recreation therapists, do. Sue and I have a great friendship that has carried us through many difficult times in both our lives. We provide one another with hope, compassion, empathy, and support. Being a resident writer in this book has enhanced her life tremendously.

Since my internship at ROP, I have remained close with several residents, and have continued to build a rapport with them. I have discovered a new friend, one man in particular. It wasn't always easy. At first, I was faced with several barriers and encountered my own fears and stigma which I had not realized existed within me. He kept to himself and rarely left his room. Consequently, this fear of the unknown made me anxious and nervous to meet this mysterious man. Many thoughts and feelings raced through my mind which were upsetting and frustrating to me. *Is he violent? Should I be alone with him? Why does he isolate himself? I am afraid.* At the time, I never thought I had the capability of having these thoughts and feelings toward another person, and it worried me. The only thing I could do was to attempt to meet and get to know him. When I first met him, he didn't want anything to do with me. He would yell at me to leave, shut the door in my face, go back to bed, and hope I'd go away. Each day, for months, I would knock on his door hoping for a different response, but I would receive the same answer. There were several times I thought of giving up. I was convinced he just didn't want to see me. However, I persevered. Although it was initially discouraging, I would go to see him as often as I could. One day, I knocked on his door expecting the usual response but, this time, he opened it with a big smile. Over time, we created a rare, but special bond. Every time I would knock on his door, he accepted my invitation with open arms and a huge smile on his face. He also had a hidden talent. Every time I visited with him, he thoroughly enjoyed playing guitar and singing for me in his room. Although our time spent together was brief, it reminded me that he is a person with thoughts and feelings of his own, and enjoys sharing his talents and interests. All it took was one person to say hello, and this experience and friendship changed both our lives forever. The stigma, fear, and prejudice I had felt prior, had vanished. He taught me that beneath the exterior, there's a special person inside. This person is not always easy to find, but because I continued the search, I realized that he had a wonderful gift to share.

Many of the residents at ROP share their talents, interests, and skills daily. They write poems and short stories, and draw and paint beautiful unique artwork. They also read, sing and dance. Some even know how to do complex computer programming and coding! Most are able to step beyond stigma and prejudice, and illustrate their talents by performing in activities such as

Interpretive Propeller Dance, singing at various special events, or displaying their art work at the Royal Ottawa Mental Health Centre. Many residents also love doing research on the Internet to further their education and learn more about their own interests. They have overcome so many obstacles by finding their passion and are creating meaningful and fulfilling lives for themselves.

At ROP, I have met some of the most compassionate, respectful, understanding, and caring people I know, and feel truly blessed and honoured to have been able to work with them. They have enriched my life tremendously.

Joann Luna

Registered Practical Nurse

I am one of the blessed nurses lucky enough to work at ROP. I was first introduced to mental health in 2009. I had the pleasure of doing my high school co-op placement in the Recreation Department. This was the time I fell in love with ROP. The staff and residents were so welcoming. I felt like I was part of a family. I went on to study nursing and completed my consolidation at ROP, and was then hired as a casual staff member in 2011.

Royal Ottawa Place has inspired me to live each day to the fullest, to always find joy in the little things, and to be thankful and grateful for what I have. The residents at ROP have brought joy into my life. I love being around them, talking and laughing with them. I have this feeling inside that I am making a difference in their lives. Each and every one of them has left a footprint in my heart. It's hard to pinpoint my favourite moment, as there are so many. One that comes to mind was our 2015 Christmas party. My team members and I danced hand-in-hand with our beloved residents. This memory still puts a smile on my face to this day. One of my most recent challenges was when a resident of mine was diagnosed with cancer. She told me about it, and it brought tears to my eyes. I felt angry wondering how someone so kind could be burdened with such a terrible thing. Late in our conversation, she was actually the one consoling me and telling me, "It's going to be okay. I'm going to get through this." I had never seen her so strong and so selfless. I felt selfish at this moment, that as her nurse, she was the one consoling me. I consider her as family and this circumstance has made me realize how strong our bond has become.

Negative thinking is still predominant in society when it comes to our attitudes surrounding mental illness. *People are mad; people are dangerous.* I often have to defend my residents to fight against this stigma. In my residents, I see the opposite. They are actually happier than those people with perfect health and money. They see the good in others. None of them would ever hurt a fly. They are outspoken and they are talented in so many ways. They have learned to live to the best of their abilities, despite illness, and have learned a multitude of coping strategies. One of my residents has even travelled the world and performed in theatre. Illness has never held her back. My residents are remarkable. They continue to impress me every single day. I am so proud of them.

Patricia Percival

Personal Care Attendant

I have been a Personal Care Attendant for 25 years. For the past 10 years, I have been working in mental health. During those 10 years, I have experienced a lot of different situations. Some are good, some not so good. During these difficult times, there is nothing more fulfilling than being able to reach out and help those in need of insight and guidance. I enjoy being part of their lives and leaving a positive footprint. Here, at ROP, we have become a family to each other, staff and residents alike. I have had the privilege to experience and to see residents play a part in each other's lives, during good or bad times. I have seen them cry, laugh, hug, break down, and sometimes be unable to cope. But at the end of the day, they always try to encourage and bring out the best in each other. There are things in our daily lives that we take for granted. Sometimes, little things, as simple as getting dressed, are a challenge. These can be difficult tasks, sometimes taking all day for someone who is struggling. In time, these tasks can be accomplished with a lot of encouragement, understanding, and devotion. It's much like planting a seed and watching it grow into a beautiful flower. Staff play a big role in handling different situations each and every day, and each new day brings different challenges. Personally, I find every moment rewarding. It fills my heart with both happiness and sadness at the same time. I feel blessed to have made an impact, and will continue to make a difference in the lives I encounter.

Veronique Hibbard

Volunteer

When I started volunteering at ROP, I doubted that I would do more than the six months minimum I had originally committed myself to. I have now been volunteering for over 10 years! Looking back, I realize that it was not just me who had to get used to dealing with the residents, but it was also the residents who had to get used to me. I was the newcomer and a certain mistrust was obvious when residents confronted me with "You are useless." or "You are stalking me." or "Don't talk to me!"

As the residents gradually accepted me, a mutual trust was built, and they opened up, first with casual conversations, followed by their life stories. What an eye-opener for me! I managed to get some residents to participate in group programs, something they had previously resisted, preferring instead to stay alone in their rooms. Working one-on-one with residents, I noticed that they were highly intelligent and creative. They often initiated a conversation by commenting on my appearance, "You look nice in yellow." or "You got your hair cut." They were also grateful for occasional chocolate treats.

Reflecting on all of these years, and on the changes I have seen in my rapport with the residents at ROP, I realize that the initial mistrust they had in me was due to the fact that, because of their mental illness, they had experienced discrimination and bias, often going back to childhood. They had been stigmatized, made fun of, and were often abandoned, even by their family members. Society turned away from them out of fear and disgust, and many ended up on the street, only to be exploited and further marginalized.

When talking about my work at ROP, friends and acquaintances often confront me with comments and questions like, "It must be difficult to work with such people." or "Don't you get depressed?" or "Aren't you afraid?" or "Have you ever been attacked?" This clearly shows that there is a widespread misconception about people with mental illness.* As an example, the Royal Ottawa Mental Health Centre was recently mentioned to me as *"the place where the feeble-minded are"*. This was from a person who had a PhD! Hearing such comments gives me an opportunity to educate ill-informed people about those who have mental illness. Those suffering with mental illness are, most often, highly intelligent people. I never fail to add that a mental illness can strike anybody, at any age, something not everybody likes to hear.

It is quite clear that mental illness is still an uncomfortable subject to talk about. Thankfully, much is being done to educate the general public. That's what we are trying to do here. Many schools, police forces, and various organizations are willing to listen to experts on the subject, often complemented by input from those who suffer themselves. Hopefully, the near future will look brighter for the afflicted, thanks to these efforts. Those who have a mental illness deserve to be treated with respect and dignity, just like anyone else.

A large number of studies have shown that very few mental illness sufferers are violent. They are often on the receiving end of violence.

Sandra Whitmore

Personal Support Worker

Sandra is a PSW at Royal Ottawa Place, and has worked there for several years. Beautifully written by Sandy is our opening poem about Nathalie Robillard, our inspiration, a woman who impacted all of us.

WE EACH HAVE A VOICE
ROP RESIDENT WRITERS

"We found hope through writing. Hear our stories and be inspired to share your own."

Chris Nihmey

"I would like to be remembered as a person who wanted to be free ... so other people would be also free."

Rosa Parks

PART I

HOPE AND INSPIRATION

"Everything that is done in the world is done by hope."

Martin Luther

YOU MEANT SO MUCH
January 11, 2011

Sandra Whitmore

You meant so much to all of us.
You were special and that's no lie.
You brightened up the darkest day,
And the cloudiest sky.

Your smile alone warmed hearts,
Your laugh was like music to hear.
We would have given anything
To have you well and standing near.

Not a moment passes
When you're not on our minds.
Your love we will never forget,
The hurt will ease in time.

Many tears we have seen and cried,
They have all poured out like rain.
We know that you are happy now,
And no longer in any pain.

Rest in peace.

Nathalie Robillard
(1977 – 2011)

LONG SHADOW
May 2009

Judy Evans

The long shadow makes patterns on the sand,
A mosaic, a kaleidoscope of beautiful life so grand.
I am so happy, content, to be in this land.
To stand, to walk, to help, to give friends a hand.
To love unconditionally, spontaneously,
On demand.
To live long, jubilant, listening to my radio,
A melodious band.
I cannot change a single grey hair strand on my head.
By the cold wind outside fanned,
Give me, good God, peace, freedom in life,
In love, forevermore, beyond end.

FLUFFY
July 2011

Sue Racine

Whenever I came home, Fluffy would be at my door barking, jumping up and down with a silly expression on her face. Her eyes would be wide open with delight, her tongue hanging out the side of her mouth. She had the most wide, infectious smile. She would try to lure me to the sofa to cuddle up or play, or, sometimes a little of both. It didn't seem to matter how long I had been away. Fluffy was just as excited to see me, as if I'd been gone all day, even if I'd just gone for a few hours to shop.

Fluffy was petite, part Maltese, part Spaniel, and her body was so warm and loving. Her two-and-a-half-foot-long body, and foot-long legs, would be snuggled around my feet and legs at night. She never snored. However, she did sometimes flail her legs about and growl in her sleep. It was as if she were trying to protect me in her slumber. Even in her dreams, Fluffy's thoughts were of me. Fluffy even went so far as to allow Snowball, my cat, to sleep on my legs, making sure that half of my leg space was available for her.

I imagine that Snowball wasn't too happy when Fluffy would have one of her legs thrashing in a growling dream. But, realizing that Fluffy was very intelligent (and a somewhat jealous dog), maybe those very active dreams weren't dreams at all. No matter how tumultuous the night was, I was always awakened every morning with several big wet kisses on my cheek.

Twenty years have come and gone since Fluffy went to Doggy Heaven. But, in my mind, I'll always see her big silly smile, her panting, off-side tongue, giving those deep loving sloppy kisses.

HEAVEN AWAITS ME
August 2014

Karen Lemieux

Jesus, you are my rock and my salvation.
On your rock, I will stand forevermore.
Like the flowers sprouting up, you created me in your
image.
You live in me, and I in you, like rain falls from Heaven.
I love you so.
The wind blows to and fro, the grass withers, and with
your arms around me, you're like a blanket of snow.
Casting all my cares upon you, you love me so, that
you stretched out your arms upon a cross to die for
me.
Heaven awaits me, your promises abound.
Wait for me at the right hand side of your Father.
Someday I will surely see you come in clouds to get
me.

LENDING A HAND, AGAIN AND AGAIN
A Fictional Children's Story
March 2012

Judy Evans

Fall, 1964, Oklahoma City, an inner-city school …

It was 10 o'clock, Monday morning recess. The bell rang and all the children ran out into the schoolyard to play. It was a warm fall day. The leaves were changing colour. The kids jumped around to different activities in the yard. Some played hopscotch, others played tag, and several students ran to the play structure.

On one of the swings was a girl named Judy. She loved the swings, just as much as jumping rope. Today she decided to use the swings. On a nice dry day, they were so much fun. You could skip in the rain, but swing? Not really. She hated wet sand. Yuck!

"Hooray! This is fun!" she yelled out to a friend who was swinging beside her. Grade 4 was full of great things, and this was something she would never forget: the wind in her hair, the look upward to the heavens. Well, all of this joy was about to change, and Judy did not notice the danger that lurked behind her.

Out of the blue, without notice, a boy suddenly appeared. His name was Dennis. He was a grade 6 student who, for some reason, did not like Judy. He always picked on her. He bullied her often in the schoolyard, and it was so unfair. She had done nothing to provoke this. Judy was friendly to everyone, but Dennis took advantage of her kindness, and her fear of telling anyone about her troubles. That would only mean more trouble for her; she just knew it. Dennis came from a troubled home where he lived with his mom and two older brothers. It was said that his oldest brother, Tom, had taken on the father role, but with poor social skills and a mean temper. Dennis often feared his nightly actions. The sound he remembered most was the slow tiptoes through the hallway to go to the bathroom, hoping to avoid any confrontation with his often-inebriated brother. This would bring many uncomfortable encounters. Dennis was known to have many bruises on his body, but he never played sports.

He walked up behind Judy, and in a mischievous voice, said, "I'm gonna push you off this swing, just like last time." He went on to laugh at her and poke at her back with every swing that came his way.

"Please, no! Leave me alone ... please!" Judy pleaded.

"No, I'm going to push you right off this swing!" Judy could hear evil pouring out of his mouth as he taunted and teased her. "I'm doing this, even if it's the last thing I ever do! Ha-ha!" He was a one-of-a-kind bully, malicious and conniving. With that, he moved in for the push. With a hard push, Judy flew off the swing and landed on her bare knees. She immediately started to cry as Dennis continued to laugh and tease.

Judy stood up and wiped sand off her legs. Nancy, the girl beside her, hopped off her swing and helped Judy to stand up. The two of them looked silently at Dennis who was proud of what he had done. They said nothing and Judy and her friend headed into the school. Judy was crying, a lot. She had a scrape on her knee and it was starting to bleed. Some other kids on the playground saw the whole thing. They watched the two girls head inside. They also watched Dennis poke around with a few other grade 6 boys, proud of what he had accomplished.

Both girls explained the story to the school nurse as she treated Judy's hurt and scraped knee. Nancy brought her into the office. Since Judy was not going to mention Dennis' name out of fear of retaliation, Nancy spoke up. "Dennis bullied her. He pushed her off the swings! She never saw it coming. Some other kids around the schoolyard saw it also. They can confirm what happened." Judy swallowed and became tense. She now feared that Dennis would come after her. Like any grade 4 student at a school facing the "big bad wolf", she feared for her life. He had instilled that type of fear in her, with his repetitive acts of bullying.

Dennis was called in from the yard. He was sent immediately to the principal's office, and upon passing Judy and Nancy, he stared them both down and punched a fist into his hand. Then the door closed and they could no longer see him. This had happened so many times before, with other students as well. Dennis was not a nice boy, and he showed this in many ways. The push off the swing was only one of the ways Judy had experienced his cruel behaviour. Inside, Dennis was warned by the principal that this was not to happen again. One more time, and he would be suspended. The principal was at the end of his rope with this rugged boy. Couldn't he just play football with the other kids? Dennis had other intentions, and they didn't involve throwing a stupid ball around. As he stepped out of the office, he began immediately to plan his next move. That's how bullies think and operate, and Dennis was one fine bully: one of the best. Practice makes perfect. But was this the "perfect" that would get him places? Dennis was convinced it would.

A few days later, after getting away with several other incidents like the swing, Dennis did not show up at school. Judy was beyond relieved, happy that she would be able to relax and have fun again at recess. It did not last. The following Monday, unfortunately, he did return. That was when something very strange happened.

Morning recess. Dennis ran out to toss a football with the others boys in his class. For some odd reason, he spent the entire recess with his classmates. He did not bully anyone. For Judy, it felt like a first; it felt like a huge relief. She couldn't believe it! Nancy couldn't believe it! No one could. He had finally spent a recess without pestering the other kids. Judy smiled when the bell rang and the two of them headed in together, happy for once that nothing had hurt them.

They felt as free as butterflies for the first time in who knew how long, maybe ever? It was a feeling that Judy remembers as she thinks back to those trying days: days that should have been remembered as the "good old days". Was there a chance that the difficult days would one day transform into days she could remember fondly? She doubted it but, that morning, for the first time, she felt a small bit of hope. The smallest of small ... realistically. After all, it was only October. It was a long year, and if last year was any indication of what this year would bring, she stayed pessimistic. These were memories that no young girl should ever have to experience.

"You've proved that you can be trusted out in the schoolyard now, Dennis."

The words continued to echo in her mind as they stepped out of the cloakroom. She gulped, grabbed Nancy, and they headed out back.

"I'm really worried, Nancy. They are letting him come out more now."

"I'm here for you, Judy. We'll stay side by side."

Throughout the week, things continued to change. It was very peculiar. At lunchtime on Friday, all the kids raced out into the beautiful leaf-filled yard. The air was warm. All the kids were excited, as they always were on a Friday. It was almost the weekend ... again! Yippee!

On the playground, a grade 6 student, Arthur, started to play his own game of tripping others with his large black boot. He was being a bully, like Dennis. This was not normal for him. Arthur was genuinely a good kid, did well in school, and came from a well-to-do family. But lately his father was struggling financially, and Arthur was the brunt of many jokes at school when his "not so appetizing" lunch was brought out to a chorus of giggles. Sandwiches were meant to have two slices of bread, and something in between. This attention was not fair, but Arthur sucked it up and tried hard to ignore and excuse his classmates' whispers and rumours. Even if this meant spending much of the lunch hour in the washroom, the place he felt most safe. Lately, his behaviour had been changing, and not for the better.

"Ha, ha, ha, take that! I hate girls, stupid girls! How do you like that?"

As he continued to pester the children on the playground, the teacher on duty started to come toward him but, as Judy looked closer, she realized that the person approaching was actually Dennis.

"Hey, leave that kid alone!"

"No, I hate her. I'll do it again and again! What are you gonna do about it?"

"I'll report you to the teacher and you won't be allowed on the playground again. Trust me, I know what you're doing, but it is not the way to make yourself feel better. Besides, I learned the hard way last week. Go ask my mom!"

"Huh?"

"I'm a bully sometimes, too, but I'm trying to change. I finally learned my lesson and now, instead of hurting, I'm helping those being bullied by others."

When Dennis, the toughest kid in the school spoke up, people listened, mostly in fear. But now, he was using his brute strength to intimidate those who wished to do harm. It really was amazing! Arthur looked at Dennis and had a change of heart. He swallowed, looked up to the sky, and then above Dennis' head.

"I really do appreciate my playground time." He dug his foot into the sand and put his hands in his pockets. "Please don't report me. I don't want to get suspended. Your mom scared you ... my mom will kill me!" Arthur tore off as the recess bell rang.

The children sighed, stared at the school and huffed and puffed their way inside. Classes resumed as normal. Their English teacher asked them a few questions. They'd been studying a poem by Judith Evans. They then started to read some mystery stories like Agatha Christie for kids. She was so great!

Dennis seemed to have changed since the last incident in the yard the previous week. Something had clicked in his head: something that made a difference to all the kids, but mostly Dennis. It was really quite amazing, almost miraculous. He had really pulled his socks up, was behaving more responsibly, and was not causing trouble like he was accustomed to doing. The teachers felt that he had improved greatly, especially in French class, where quite often things were difficult. The transformation was not complete, but at least it had started, Judy hoped. It was clear that things were turning the right way. Maybe his run-in with Judy had changed his life ... it definitely changed hers. She had to agree with these facts! She had not lost a strand of hair all week and her pants were free of mud!

Catherine was the toughest girl in grade 6. She was not friendly and also came from a difficult home. You might say her life was "impossible". She had a lot of issues at school, not only in her grades, but also with her peers. This caused her to say and do things that were not rational. She always felt anxious, frustrated and, at times, this led her to be mean to those around her. It was very sad, but Catherine was known as the dirty kid, the kid to stay away from, but these titles paled in comparison to what she was becoming ... a bully, trying to compensate for her shortcomings.

It was morning recess, a week following Dennis' confrontation with Arthur. The kids weaved, bobbed, and scurried into the yard. It was another beautiful fall day. It was not cold, but not warm either. The majority of kids kept their coats on, except for the brave grade sixers! The birds were flying high and the odd, "Look, look!" accompanied the Canada Geese flying south, as they honked loudly. Catherine was looking up and pointing. She noticed the younger kids doing the same. She had an idea. She wanted to do something mean. She just felt it in her body, with memories of her father's escapade the night before. It was a night she would never forget. The bruise would heal, but the scar was deeper. Her anger and frustration had risen to the top. It was her time to take revenge. On her father? Never, he was too strong. And, after all, he was her father, and she loved him. Didn't she?

"You don't deserve to be in the playground, kid! Kids like you shouldn't be here!" she yelled at a grade 3 student.

"But, we want to play. You can't tell us we can't play. Leave us alone."

Catherine started to raise her voice. "You want a good time? What about me? I want a good time, too! And that will happen, when I push you! Hey! That rhymes!"

Relaxing under a tree, Arthur woke to the ruckus on the playground. The arguing continued and Catherine was really loud. She was yelling and pointing her finger in the boy's face. She was stopping the kids from using the swings. Arthur stood up and made his way over to Catherine. He remembered the words of wisdom that Dennis had spoken the previous week.

"Hey Cat, treat your neighbour as you want to be treated. You don't know that? Stop yelling, you're hurting my ears! Look what happened to me last week. I was on the playground, just like you. Dennis caught me bullying some helpless grade 4's. He taught me a lesson that day that kept me from being suspended. Do

you want to face your dad? You know what he's like …
I'm telling you, Cat, it just isn't the way."

"But, freakoid, I like the way I am. This IS the way.
I don't care. Just leave me alone. I do what I want! My
dad does what he wants!"

"Yah, but look at him. You want to be like that? You
want to be him? If you don't stop being mean, you will
be suspended and you'll realize it is just not worth the
hassle. If you continue, it will happen, again and again.
Dennis taught me to treat others the way I want to be
treated. It's really working, Cat. Trust me on this."

To Catherine, it seemed like a simple message, but
it finally hit home and she calmed down. She stopped
yelling and walked away with Arthur who put an arm
around her shoulder. The kids heard them talking. "It
will get better." She dropped her head and replied, "I
hope so."

A cycle began that fall at Liverpool Elementary. It
was a trend that carried a simple message about
treating people well. It took one person to appreciate its
importance and, like dominoes, it continued. From
Dennis to Arthur to Catherine, a cycle of reaching out to
one person at a time began to move forward. It made
the schoolyard a better place, a safer place, a happier
place.

Catherine, Dennis, and Arthur finally graduated.
They all moved on to higher grades at other schools.
Judy always wondered if the changes would continue.
They may have moved on, but not before planting the
seeds in their elementary school: seeds of change.
They would be seeds of hope for better days, helping
kids to see others equally and treat each other well.
These seeds would not only begin to grow in the
playground, but also in the hearts of those who had
moved on, like Dennis, like Arthur, like Catherine.
Those who had suffered within, but had reached for
more. Judy was amazed by the changes in her school,

and hoped these seeds would continue to be planted year after year.

As is always the case, the future would roll forward. Judy and her classmates would graduate from grade 6 and begin new paths, new journeys, some hopeful, others hurtful. Life wasn't always "hunky dory". She knew that, as did other graduates who came from difficult pasts.

Years have rolled on at Liverpool Elementary. Judy remembers her days fondly, but especially the change that happened, within herself, and within her schoolmates, sparked by the choices made by kids who struggled: kids who managed to find a spark within themselves. When this spark was combined with other sparks, a flame developed and was passed on year after year. A pact would be made in 1964 by a group of students who would make a difference, who would say to themselves, *"What am I doing?"*, and make a change.

To this day, if you walk through Liverpool Elementary, where their lives transformed, where echoes of past achievements and success ring through the hallways, you will stumble upon a special plaque hanging in a glass case by the playground doors. It is a special symbol representing the choices made by each student at Liverpool from 1964 on. From that year forward, students swore a pact and made this promise:

Our school is a bully-free zone, a place of acceptance, a place of love, a place free from discrimination. It is a place where differences are not only accepted, but also valued, celebrating the special qualities we all possess and share with others.

If you look very closely at the plaque, you will also notice something very special inscribed beside it. It is a message of hope from someone who, at the time, was making his own change in the world: a vision of love and compassion for mankind, regardless of their differences. A man who would go on to change the way we perceive our neighbours, so that no one would be judged by how they look, or where they come from. His name: Martin Luther King Jr. Prior to his assassination in 1967, he visited the inner-city school after hearing about its transformation. He was so proud of the school's initiative and challenge to get rid of bullying forever. Upon his visit, he commended the students of Liverpool on the positive change they had committed to make. From that day forward, the school was renamed, MK Elementary.

The days of Dennis and Arthur and Catherine are over. Judy's days have long passed. But one thing remains true at MK Elementary, as it approaches its 50th anniversary. This special plaque encased in glass and the message from this great leader have been cherished year after year, student after student. Even today, before any student exits the doors into the playground, each student will take a quick glance to the left and promise to make their schoolyard a better place: a place of acceptance and compassion. It has become a place to embrace uniqueness, while also realizing that we're not so different after all.

Has bullying disappeared completely? Of course not. Kids are kids, they are learning, they are growing, they are changing. But when bullying occurs at MK, it is caught, goodness is taught, and the school becomes a much safer place. In helping one another, these values have become priceless. May this message live on, from here and beyond.

PART II

PERSEVERANCE AND HEALING

"The greatest glory in living lies not in never falling, but in rising every time we fall."

Nelson Mandela

A BIOGRAPHY OF JUDY EVANS
February 2012

Chris Nihmey

I am writing this on behalf of Ms. Judy Evans. I have known this intelligent, charismatic, and wonderful person for the past three years, while volunteering at her residence, Royal Ottawa Place. For three very productive years, not only has Judy continued to battle through her ailments, she has worked with me continuously, writing poems and stories for readers of all ages. It has been very therapeutic for her healing. And every opportunity not only helps her with her writing but, more importantly, her well-being. I have been touched by someone whose strong character, strength, motivation, and perseverance through difficult times have made her a model of faith, determination and courage. I feel truly blessed to have Judy in my life.

July 4, 1945, in Toronto, Ontario, Judith Evans came into the world, a beautiful baby girl, vibrant, and full of energy. Her father, a diplomat who worked in a different country every two years, moved his family for much of Judy's early life. She thus attended various schools through the years, and spent her last few years at Hillcrest High School, when the family settled in Ottawa for a time.

Judy attended Hillcrest from grades 11 to 13, graduating in 1964. Following graduation, the family moved to Cleveland, Ohio, where Judy took the SATs and did very well. She was accepted to Western Missouri University, set to major in English and Art History. Life was looking up for her, and the momentum of success was pushing her toward great things.

Everything looked bright and optimistic for Judy. However, following high school, something started to change within her. In her early twenties, strange and unusual things began to happen to her body and mind. These feelings were extremely uncomfortable, unwanted, and foreign to her. As they increased in intensity, she and her family started to fear the worst, and in only a short time, it happened. Judy hit a wall. An insurmountable object lay in her path: an awful, terrible obstacle. At the age of 22, Judy was diagnosed with Paranoid Schizophrenia, a debilitating disease of the mind, one of the worst one can experience. It would change her life forever. A shadow would loom over her many proud accomplishments and awards. She would now, forever, be labelled: sick. At the time, for Judy, it was more than a sickness. It was a diagnosis of death.

Her plans for becoming a teacher were quickly dismissed, when merely waking up and getting through her breakfast was the toughest of challenges: next to impossible. How could she face the world again? With stigma increasing in society, how would the world face her? But most importantly, how could she face herself? Death was on her doorstep. She could feel it directly in front of her. It would be something she would contemplate many times. It would become an attempt to free herself from the chains … from the pain.

For the next four years, Judy was a patient at a psychiatric hospital in Kingston. She remembers the day her mother drove her there. It was a dark, depressing day. At the time, hope seemed lost. Pumped with medications, she gained excess weight, which destroyed her self-esteem and confidence. It would take a long while for her mind to accept that these little pills were meant to help her. Lacking the will or even the strength to exercise or be active in any way, she spent day after day lying in bed, staring at the ceiling, fighting intrusive thoughts. When sleeping, traumatic dreams would wake her to the reality that she was completely alone. She was left with only her destructive thoughts, delusions, hallucinations, and psychosis. Her mind would not find hope or freedom for a long time.

Through many difficult years, from minimal improvements, to simple jobs that seemed to take her nowhere, she struggled along, day after day, month after month, year after year. Success seemed a far cry from where she stood, proverbial cinderblocks around her ankles, preventing her from taking progressive steps forward. Late in her stay in Kingston, she met a man she thought she could trust and confide in. She quickly found out the hard way that this was not the case. One night, the two of them made a quick and quiet escape from the hospital, where a car awaited. They escaped the confines of the hospital, heading west to Trenton. This effort to break down the walls surrounding her was quickly shaken when police officers found her. She was thrown into jail. In her state, and with her diagnosis, she was seen as a threat to society, and was labelled an outcast. Though she was finding some improvement in her state of mind, and was taking small steps forward, she was still viewed as an "accident waiting to happen". She was returned to Kingston, a place she found so difficult. However, in short order, in what was a miraculous turn of events, she was transferred to Ottawa, where she was to spend much time at the Royal Ottawa Mental Health Centre. It was there that her blessings would be counted.

Medication, exercise, mental strategies, a competent therapist: all would come into play over the years, as she found greater improvements in her thinking. Thoughts that would normally consume her mind and leave her feeling isolated within, were now being destroyed with more positive thoughts and actions, which built a much more stable life for her. More importantly, a stable mind.

In 2006, with undying perseverance and a desire to live again, and heal, Judy was now healthy enough to move from the ROMHC into Royal Ottawa Place, a residence housing over 100 people, each suffering from a variety of mental and physical challenges. It was a move that Judy longed to find for far too long. Her desire, her will, and her competency finally emerged. She could not have been happier. Although it was the longest of roads to get there, she knew that she was taking greater strides. She prayed this would continue and trusted God to carry her to solid ground.

Since 2006, Judy has lived at ROP. She is doing extremely well, thriving as a youthful 70-year-old. She continues to move forward, pushing away the ailments and struggles by bounding over the hardships in her way. She has emphasized many times over, after all these years, that she finally feels safe. It has made her the person she is today—a proud, confident and passionate woman. She can now face herself each morning when she combs her hair and washes her face. She finally agrees that the woman in the mirror is the "real" her, not the horrible monster she once saw.

I can attest that Judy is a kind, competent, goal-driven individual, and a writer who wants her poems and stories to reach out, here and beyond. She told me one day, "Chris, please take these poems to the classrooms you teach in. Read my words to them so that they can be inspired. It is then that I will have accomplished my goal of being a teacher. Through you, my dream to teach will come true." Well, her dream has come true. I have spoken to different students and classes, and the responses to her poems have been overwhelming. It has been a true test of her story of courage and redemption.

Please read Judy's entries and consider them, not just as poems and stories, but her reason for living; they are her message, her tale, her treacherous, yet inspiring journey. As with all journeys in life, there are ups and downs, hills and valleys. But in the end, it does not matter whether you stand on a hill or in a valley. What matters is, that either way, you've kept on "trucking" forward. Life is not always about succeeding. It is about trying and never giving up, no matter what life puts in your path. Judy has done this. She has finally found true peace and happiness within her, something so pure that she has never experienced before.

When I look at Judy today, it is clear that she sees something that so many of us fail to see in life. It is called hope and, although it seemed lost at one time, she has finally been reunited with it. This is the reason she wakes up each morning with the drive and desire to open her door, and reach out to someone who may be in similar shoes. Mental illness is not the end. It is an obstacle that, once crossed, can lead one to live a fulfilling and satisfying life.

How deep can our thoughts take us? Deep enough to die, but that was not in the plan for Judy. She chose to continue to heal and live again, and our world is blessed because of it.

HAWKS DESTINY: An Autobiography
September 2013

Beverley Sunday

Life is not the same anymore. I've had to learn how to walk again, use my left hand again, and talk correctly again. It has been hard work to do everything all over. In 2010, my life changed forever.

Before my accident, I had visions of doing great things. I was planning on opening a fitness studio. I was working as a personal trainer and fitness instructor. It was a dream come true. I had also participated in the 2010 Winter Olympics as one of the Indigenous dancers. Now … I have to start all over again. Everything I did, like dancing at the Olympics, was on my own. I learned all by myself. I met the right people to help me. I believe it was supposed to be that way. Now, I'm dealing with a bigger challenge in my life: putting myself back together with the help of The Creator. I hope He helps me because I need His help now, more than ever.

My injury changed my life completely. This life experience has been rough. I had so many dreams of being independent, having my own business, and being rich. I still plan to do it, but I have a bigger challenge now. I just need to keep focused and think about my children a lot more: Aerial, Jamila and Kalid.

I must say, I believe in God more now because I'm still alive. I was so close to dying. I wasn't ready to die. I often think back to the life I once had. Life was a whole lot different in many ways.

I was adopted at the age of six months by a family on a reserve near St. Paul, Alberta. My biological mom's brother was the chief at the time, so that was good for me. My biological dad was Métis and lived about 30 minutes from my reserve. I didn't meet him until I was twelve! I wasn't brought up traditionally. I was put into a school off the reserve. It wasn't a good thing to be native at this school. It created huge problems.

My mom never really taught us how to creatively design, and to dance at powwows. She taught us how to be tough so we could stick up for ourselves. I mean, urbanized, because I was brought up on the reserve. The city was a whole new thing for me.

Twelve was a weird kind of age for me. The only close sister I had was Wanda, my adopted sister. The other sisters I had were older and had their own lives: married with children.

In our elementary school years, Wanda and I went to school together. This continued in intermediate and high school. We used to walk to elementary school if we missed the bus. It was about two miles from our house.

On our reserve, we used to walk up to the Cardinal's store, where I first met Lance who worked there. Aerial, my first child, was actually conceived with Lance, which was not good. I was only 12 at the time! He was 18. I lost my virginity to him. Afterward, he became very abusive and jealous, and I actually put up with him until I was 18.

We used to meet at the park and go fishing together. I'd help him clean the store. I eventually got a job at the store as a gas jockey and cashier. I worked there until I graduated from high school. After graduation, at the "mature" age of 19, I was making plans to travel to Edmonton for college to be on my own. It was a big decision. I didn't really decide to go until I met a new boyfriend, Nathan. I met him in St. Paul, a town by the reserve, about 30 minutes away. We met at a bar. He told me that he was from Ontario and was planning to move to Edmonton. This definitely excited me! I told him of my visions and dreams. That night, I ended up giving him my cell number so we could connect when he moved to Edmonton. Once I arrived in Edmonton, he called me. We talked briefly, met up, and after a few deep discussions, and a few rash decisions, we decided to live together. Yes, it was fast, but I truly felt he was "the one for me". This did not last.

First off, we had to find an elementary school for my daughter Aerial. Thank goodness there was a school only five minutes away but, unfortunately, bad news would come my way. I was not accepted into college and, in a panic, I ended up contacting my ex-husband, Lance. He had moved to Fort Smith, Northwest Territories, for work. I decided to apply to college there. I thought it would be a good idea for Aerial to be with both her parents, in the same place. I got accepted, told Nathan my plan, but it did not go well. He was sad and disappointed. He told me he wanted to move with me. I thought that was a great idea! I confessed my love to him. I wanted to be with him forever. He felt the same way.

We moved to Fort Smith, NWT, so that I could attend Aurora College. I ended up breaking up with Nathan shortly after the move. Sadly, I ended up having to move back to St. Paul when school was done. I had completed half of my course, so I applied to go back to college in Edmonton. There, of all the people who wanted to help me get back on my feet, was Lance. He found me an apartment close to my college, and a school for Aerial.

As months went by, and things began to change in our lives, Lance applied for custody of our daughter without telling me. I realized that the love and attention he was giving me since my return was just a ploy. We would experience five years of family court and, thankfully, I would win full custody. It was a challenge, but it was nothing compared to the pain and suffering I would experience years later.

And then … there was Joe. Who would have thought? I met Joseph at a bar in St. Paul. He would eventually become the father of my other two children: Jamila and Kalid. That night, we found ourselves dancing and, yes, drinking. He told me he was from Montreal, Quebec. He told me he ended up in St. Paul because he and his uncle had purchased a hotel. This interested me and we ended up visiting his hotel. He was driving a Mercedes so, right away, I thought, okay, he's not poor.

In all honesty, upon seeing the hotel, I thought it looked very cheap. We discussed all kinds of things that night. I told him about the rights I had as a native, and what life was like back on my reserve. He wanted to come see the reserve, so I told him to come the next day. I took him on a tour. I even took him to my mom's house to introduce him to my family. Surprisingly, during my time on the reserve, my mom had decided to give me a piece of her land. I gladly accepted.

So Aerial now had another stepdad. All I wanted was a stable guy, but, even early on, Joseph and I weren't doing the best. He was an avid smoker and a pot head. I got into the habit as well, but not every day like him. He was bugging me a lot about buying a trailer and moving it to the land I was given, but it was not a dream of mine to live on the reserve … broke.

Then it happened again. I got pregnant for the second time and gave birth to another daughter, Jamila, in October of 1997. I now had two daughters and all I kept thinking was, holy crap, what did you do? I ended up having my third kid in November of 1998. This time it was a boy, so although I was happy to have another child, I was completely stressed out. I had three kids, I was still not married and … I was still poor.

Years would pass, things would change, but not always for the good. In 2005, we decided to move to Ottawa. Finally, my new beginning was going to happen. Life had changed in many ways. I became very health oriented and I wanted to open the first Aboriginal fitness studio in Ottawa. I started to work for Odawa Native Friendship Centre as the health coordinator. I was given the chance to know more natives, which is what I wanted. It was a homerun for me.

My house was in a perfect location. It was close to my work, and Aerial's school. I really thought my life was coming together, finally. I wanted to become a personal trainer and fitness instructor. Odawa knew I had bigger goals, so they hired me and I used their facility to help me reach my goals. My pay would increase once I became certified as a personal trainer and fitness instructor. It meant work, work and more work. So, I designed workouts for the community and finally became certified as a personal trainer. My next goal was to become a fitness instructor. Odawa allowed me to get trainers to come use our facility to train me.

In 2010, a wonderful opportunity came my way. I was chosen to dance at the Winter Olympics. I was thrilled, but I needed to learn how to dance, and what kind of dance I would use. My long-term goals were coming together finally. Except … Joe. We were not doing well together. We were still arguing constantly.

During my work, I met a guy from Toronto. His name was Steve and he was good looking and had a good job. At the time, Joe was doing contract work in Montreal with his family. I still wasn't happy with him, with us. I decided to go. I arranged my kids' schedules with Joe. I was gone for a couple of days to Toronto. I got hold of Steve. I told him my plans and he was as excited as I was. He rented a motel room for those two days. We did end up sleeping together. I knew it was not a good thing. I was scared to go face Joe now, but how could I hide this?

I got back to Ottawa and we continued to fight. To get it off my chest, I ended up telling Joe that I cheated on him. We slept in different rooms that night, and that became our life for a while.

February 19, 2010. The day I want to forget, but can't.

I remember that Joe and I were travelling back from Gatineau to Ottawa. We were arguing about everything. I was driving the car and, I mean it, we were really arguing! I lost control. We drove into a ditch and then hit a tree ... blackness.

We were taken to the hospital, both having experienced serious brain injuries. I lost my kids. I lost my licence. I lost everything, even my dignity.

I've had very little family support on my end. I feel I've lost all my kids now. I have had to learn everything all over again, with no family around me. It's very difficult and depressing.

I have now lost custody of all my children, but my kids are well taken care of. I have had to rebuild myself all over again. It's tiring sometimes, but I can't give up until, one day, I have a big ceremony and walk again, waving the hand that I've lost movement in. In the future, I want to find a good husband, too. The right guy for me.

Since the accident in 2010, I've been to four different facilities to get me back on my feet. The first one was Robin Easey Centre. I also lived at Grace Manor. But my last resort was moving to Royal Ottawa Place.

In 2010, I finally got a chance to meet my first elder. His name is Albert, and he would become an additional support for me. He comforted me and taught me a little bit more about the natives in the east. He's part of the Algonquin tribe, way different from mine, Cree. He is wise, talented, and comforting. I believe we were meant to meet because I was striving to be more native, and having a traditional elder was a plus. I will never let Albert go as my elder. I love him and he's done so much for me.

The hardest thing I've had to deal with is the trauma all by myself, because my family is in Alberta. Thankfully, I have now become my own Power Of Attorney. This means I can make my own decisions, which is great. My next big goal is to become my own guardian. This would mean I could handle my own expenses. It will be challenging, since the major injury to my brain affects my critical thinking. But I'll prove them wrong. I also want to get my driver's licence back one day. I am determined to succeed!

Since the accident, I've started going to therapy. I go to a gym to work on my arm, and on balance. My goal is to lose weight. My occupational therapist has given me my licence for my powered wheelchair. She stretches my weak hand, and is a wonderful comfort. I also have a speech lady who helps me with communication. Most importantly, my physiotherapist helps me with walking, balance, and using my hand. She helps me with my most critical goals. The biggest is to become more independent. I must admit, this is finally happening. I attend a health recovery class. It is soothing, calm, and relaxing, something I need to learn how to achieve within myself. I have also started to attend church. I need The Creator much, much more.

I am more determined to be independent. I recently met an author at my residence (ROP) who plans to enter my story into a book he is producing. I am very excited about it. I have to admit, things are looking up. Regardless of the annoyances, I'm finally beginning to like it here.

Who knows what life may bring?

WHAT IS YOUR LIFE ABOUT?
June 2014

Elizabeth Gervais

Eloquent

Loving

Intelligent

Zebras

Alone

Betty

Entertaining

Trust

Heaven

LIVING WITH MENTAL ILLNESS
An Autobiography
April 2013

Karen Lemieux

My name is Karen Lemieux. I was diagnosed with Bipolar Disorder in 1982. At the time, I was hospitalized for six months at the Cornwall General Hospital, Psychiatric Ward, but this story started a long time ago.

I was born and raised in Cornwall. In my home, there was always fighting. My mother wanted to be a nurse, but my parents had a lot of kids to take care of, so she couldn't be one. She took up drinking and started to bring other men into the house. She then started to take her frustrations out on us, especially me. When Children's Aid and the police found out about this, they took us kids away.

I was put in Rideau Regional Hospital in Smiths Falls. Apparently, I had emotional problems from an upsetting home life. This caused people to think I was mentally handicapped, which in those days meant I was a retard. Carrying this stigma was awful. In my first foster home, I was kept at home until I was nine years old. I then started school. When I was in school, the kids would ask where I was from. Of course, I told them. From then on, I was picked on. Things went like that until I left the school. From there on, I just hushed up about where I came from, and I started to act differently. I was actually in four different schools until I was 19.

At the age of 12, I made my first trip to the Cornwall General to see my first psychiatrist. A few months later, I was admitted onto the third floor, South Psychiatric Ward. I stayed there for two months, and then began a Day Hospital program. This was a two-year program and I was in and out of the hospital daily.

I was placed into my third foster home until the age of 18. That was when I started to act strange. In January of 1982, I was admitted into the hospital again, and was there for six months. I was diagnosed with Bipolar Disorder (manic depression) and I didn't get out until June. I was put on lithium and chlorpromazine for my illness. Needless to say, my last year of high school was very rough. I couldn't concentrate, I couldn't stay awake, and I ended up having to quit school.

From there on, I was sent all over the place, from group homes to boarding homes, until the age of 21, when I was finally out on my own. That was when my biological father found me again: in my fourth foster home. I began to go see him and stay over at his place. This continued until I was 30 years old. All in all, my father was very good to me. At least he showed me that he could be a father, and that he cared. That's the way I see it. He came back into my life and I was happy. It's funny, when I was 18, he had actually promised he'd come back into my life. He had mentioned this when I was in my first foster home.

Dad eventually passed away at the age of 64, because of an ulcer in his leg. Gangrene developed. It was from a car accident he had had long ago. It spread to both his legs and through his body, and within two weeks of being hospitalized, he passed away. We really grieved dad's death, and I attended the funeral.

From 18 to 33 years of age, I was hit with another difficulty that I had to learn to live with. It was an illness that put me in a wheelchair. I attribute a lot of this to the medication I was on. It really affected my body. I tried to tell my psychiatrists that I shouldn't be on it, but they insisted I keep taking it. My boyfriend at the time took me to the hospital one day because there were spots on my body. I got inside the doors of the General Hospital in Ottawa, and collapsed. They had to resuscitate me because I was slipping away. I have no recollection of what happened from there, but six weeks later, I woke up. The diagnosis was Toxic Epidermal Syndrome (flesh-eating disease). My boyfriend was there with a good friend, and there were doctors standing around me. They told me what had happened. When I sat up, I noticed that my foot was crooked. I tried to stand but almost fell. Apparently, I had experienced a stroke. I also noticed that my left leg and left hand were lame because of the disease, combined with the stroke. When I tried eating for the first time on my own, I ended up swallowing a bunch of teeth. I was then transferred back to the Hotel Dieu Hospital in Cornwall. I was bedridden for about a year. When I was a little bit better, I could get around in a wheelchair. I went back to live at the Riverview Manor, where I was staying before everything happened.

At Riverview, things were not going well. I was angry at God, everyone else, and especially myself. I blamed God for taking away my privilege to walk. I loved to walk. I used to walk all over the place. One time, I walked right through the town of Cornwall, which was no small feat.

From then on, I built up a lot of anger, which triggered my mental illness, and I became psychotic. I was throwing chairs across the room, knocking pictures off the walls, and telling everybody off. My self-esteem went very low, and I ended up not caring about anything. I just didn't care. I felt useless in a wheelchair! All I thought about was the worst. *I'm going to be like this for the rest of my life!* My stupid club foot and lame hand! Thank God I had my right hand working again. At least I could feed myself.

I started smoking and I smoked like a chimney. I was put in the General Hospital at the Cornwall Psychiatric Ward. I was then transferred to Brockville. I just started travelling from hospitals, to institutions, and even jails; all because of my poor behaviour. My attitude and outlook on life was at an extreme low. It was so negative.

In Brockville, I had a tough time. It was awful. I hit and screamed and yelled at people. My temper tantrums were many. I ended up in a seclusion room where I just pounded the walls. Sometimes they would give me medication to calm me down. From there, I was given another label. I was labelled psychotic. I felt they just weren't dealing with my problems. In the five years I was there, it seemed like I never spoke to a nurse or a doctor. I received no answers to anything until I came to Ottawa.

I left in September of 2003, after five years. I came to live at the Royal Ottawa Mental Health Centre. I was there for the next ten months and, in June of 2004, I finally got the treatment I needed. My medications were changed. I started to see improvements. I took some courses on anger management and assertiveness training, and I was in a group where I tried to gain back my self-esteem. These all helped me a bit. That summer, I moved to Royal Ottawa Place, next door to the Health Centre. I was one of the first people to live there when it first opened in 2004.

My first six years continued to be rough. I was still having a lot of anger outbursts. Telling staff off, and slamming my bedroom door, were regular occurrences. I wanted to take programs in the community, but I was not allowed. I had to have five or six years of good behaviour before I could ever think of going into the community. I didn't have a psychiatrist until May 2010. When I first met my new psychiatrist, I liked her very much. She helped me out a great deal.

Now, in 2013, it will be three years. She suggests the pills I should take, and has given me techniques on what to do in situations to deal with my anger. When I first lived at ROP, I took a course on different coping skills. The doctor told me to use some coping skills, like deep breathing, leaving the situation to go to my room, and screaming into a pillow. I was told by a recreation therapist that I could go to my room and listen to soft music and just chill out, so that's what I did, and still do today. I also have a very strong faith life which has really helped me succeed. I've come so far in the last three years. I was given early permission to go into the community. I do so without the fear of having any outbursts or anything.

I have now been at ROP for nine years. I must say I love my home a lot! I give credit to the staff, psychiatrists, and nurses. They are awesome! My self-esteem is coming back and I'm feeling a lot better about myself. I know what to do in different situations without anyone getting hurt. Most of all, I've learned to accept the fact that I'm in a wheelchair, and may never walk again. But at least I'm alive and I can do things for myself. I have people I care for and love very much. This is my home forever. I'm on a dietary plan to try to lose fifty pounds. I continue to work at quitting smoking. I will try to overcome every obstacle I encounter. I am a fighter, a survivor, a winner, and I can do this and I'm going to make it. Why? Because I'm Karen Lemieux, I love myself, and I can do it!

This … is my life.

THE LIFE OF DICKY
November 2013

Dickens Pierre-Louis

Family name: Pierre-Louis

First name: Dickens (Dicky)

Entered ROP: 2007

Mom: Rosette

Daughter: Yedidia

Birth country: Haiti – moved to Ottawa at the age of 13

Circumstance: car accident as an adult (wheelchair for mobility)

Favourite sports: basketball, tennis, soccer

Favourite team: Chicago Bulls (NBA)

Favourite subject: English

Favourite movie: Taxi Driver

Favourite TV show: Taxi

Favourite colour: brown

Favourite food: rice, beans and chicken

Favourite dessert: ice cream

Favourite hobbies: Connect 4 (I can beat anyone!) & cars (Oh, my BMW!)

A JOURNAL CAN SPEAK A THOUSAND WORDS
August 2011

Judy Evans

August 4, 2011

A good friend told me that her psychiatrist said she is doing well. That's what my psychiatrist told me today. I am determined it shall continue. My doctor is a very good psychiatrist. I am at peace and feel at ease knowing that I am in her hands. I will probably see her again the Wednesday after next. I hope and pray she continues to tell me I am doing well. I love to hear that. I pray I live a long and happy life. That's what I really yearn for.

In July of 2011, my sister-in-law bought me a ticket to Calgary, WestJet Airlines. I stayed in Canmore, Alberta, for two weeks! It was wonderful.

I don't smoke anymore, and never will again. My mother, Audrey Evans, would be SO proud of me.

I was born in a hospital in Toronto on July 4th, 1945, at three in the morning. I gave my mother a hard time! My father was in the waiting room when he heard he had a newborn baby girl. He fainted!

I was born with pneumonia and they didn't think I'd live, so my birth certificate was not issued until ten days after I was born! I am so very happy I was born, that I lived. I hope I live a long and fruitful life.

My sister was born in 1953, in Havana, Cuba, when I was 8 years old. My father was posted there, where he worked for the Canadian government as a Trade Commissioner. He was happy to have another girl. I looked after my sister, changing her diapers, giving her baths. My mother was working as a nurse. I taught my sister to tie her shoelaces in a bow so she could go to kindergarten.

My eldest brother, Michael, was born in St. Louis, Missouri, USA. When he was 21 years old, he chose American citizenship. He is a photographer. He used to work for the New York Times! My sister has been so good to me. She's very positive and upbeat. I continue on because of her love for me. I love her so.

Wow! I am 66 years young and will always be young at heart. I love being creative, writing sonnets, and new stories. Chris, the elementary school teacher, will eventually publish my writings in a book, along with Danny Parent`s stories, and so many others.

I do like writing poems and stories, using my brain, being creative. Chris is very kind. He has read my stories to his students. They like them a lot. I always wanted to be a high school teacher (English, Drama). Sickness had other plans.

My father was posted to Cleveland, Ohio. He paid for my education. I did two years, but couldn't finish due to illness. I also studied Psychology, Freud and Jung, which was fascinating.

Each winter, I cry a little, remembering my mother who is with God now. I miss her dearly. She took her own life. I actually tried to kill myself when I was 17 years old. The wounds on my left arm healed. I never tried it again: never will again. This is my life!

I go to art class every Thursday, where I do some watercolour painting. They are semi-realistic, semi-abstract. I hope they'll all be sold one day. I love to be creative and productive.

I shall probably write more sonnets. I didn't know I could write such stories. I hope to be inspired to write more of them, on different topics. It is so good of Chris to write with us. It must be very satisfying. I know it has changed my outlook on life. Regardless of dealing with an illness that took so much away, life has brought all the right people into my life. I can be thankful for that ... Judy

PART III

LIFE AND BEAUTY WITHIN

"If you wanna make the world a better place, take a look at yourself and then make a change."

Michael Jackson
Man In The Mirror
by Ballard and Garrett

LIFE
December 2011

Judy Evans

Life must commence,
But I am dark and serious;
A mere pretence,
Against the glowing, of the coming down,
Slow, stupid, mooning of the
Comedic clown.

Against pretence.
My tears are mere trickles of complaint;
I make something into something,
More than it should be.

Chris Nihmey

ULTIMATE FLYERS FAN
September 2011

Greg Bacon

Best Ever   Perseverance   Powerful

Triumphant   Bernie Parent   Black

CARTER   Acrobatic   Strength   Puck

Orange   Hextall   East   Yes!

GO PHILLY!

2 Stanley Cups   Quick   Freedom

Hit   Hard   Hope   HELP!

Never Give Up!   PRONGER   Defense

Offense   Richards   Poke Check

IRONICALLY SPEAKING
September 1991

Laily Kant

Did you ever find yourself with a dry mouth, scared to go to a class even though you didn't have to do an oral test? Have you ever been afraid to walk into a classroom for fear of dying from the smell of rose mist air-spray? How about the age-old, stick-out-your-hand, get-slapped-by-the-ruler phobia? These fears have plagued me and the many other victims who were subject to Madame, the eccentric Egyptian-French teacher who taught me in public school.

Her classroom was no ordinary one, as I am not talking about an ordinary woman. She was given a separate portable of her own in the middle of our playground and baseball diamond. This was because the rest of the staff felt we students were better adapted to the lingering aroma of her classroom, which she religiously sprayed with rose air freshener. Consequently, we were constantly reminded of Madame's French class, even during our recesses! Mind you, it was not so much the French class, as it was Madame herself, who petrified us.

She was a rather large lady, making a point of stressing this as a very effective teaching method. Everything about her was large. Her dresses, sometimes brown with big white polka dots, sometimes red with blue polka dots, accentuated her figure most daringly. So stylish was she, that each outfit had a pair of matching eyeglass frames. I thought the nicest ones were the blue ones with the white pearls all around. She was "Elton John" minus the voice. Yet, we would all go home with Madame's famous shrill, "Qu'est-ce que tu fais là?" ringing in our ears.

We could never decide whether her looks or her teaching methods frightened us more. One had to be attentive at all times as Madame could pick you to recite *"verbe être en passé composé"*, regardless of whether you knew it or not. Your best bet was to know it, or else say goodbye to the natural colour of your palms. Madame used rulers and yardsticks of all sizes, depending on the severity of the punishment due. But if there was a difficult question to which no one knew the answer, Madame offered rewards for the correct answer, starting with a nickel, and progressing to a quarter. By that time, everyone was up on their chairs, hands elevated, with the noise level unbearable! Another reason for the portable.

Fridays were really special in French class as it was Bingo Day! Madame used to recite the letters and numbers in French, the winner receiving a prize from the treasure bin. The treasure bin was comprised of Madame's junk, which we all found fascinating. I once won an ornate silver fly brooch with diamond eyes and a pearl back. It was grotesquely real, but it was a beauty of a prize!

Students' birthdays were very special to Madame. Ironically, it would turn out to be the worst day in the student's year if Madame found out it was their birthday. She would plant a humongous kiss on your face, paying no attention to the fact that your face was turned desperately away from her. She then proceeded to choose two volunteers to give the birthday person the bumps, ignorant of the fact that the often dirty floor left terrible stains on new jeans and skirts usually worn on birthdays!

The only time we could ever take revenge on Madame was during recess and lunchtime. There were so many of us, that she could never point a finger unless one of us was caught in the act. During the spring, we used to purposely aim our baseballs at the back of

Madame's portable, knowing she would come pounding out to lash out at us with a "Qu'est-ce que tu fais là?" We always seemed to know just how much time it would take to annoy her. Thus, we were usually able to disperse into the woods before she came around. There was always one slowpoke that got dragged off by the ear to the principal's office.

Winter was the most fun for revenge, as it brought soft, packed, wet snow which was perfect snowball material. Needless to say, Madame's portable windows were the most challenging targets on the playground. It became a skillful game of hit and run! The school was built in an area with many slopes and small hills. Being the young adventuresome kids we were, shiny, slippery ice slides going down these slopes were constructed all over the playground. Madame's portable was situated at the base of the best slope. Every time someone went gliding down one of the slides, their journey inevitably ended with a huge thump on Madame's portable wall. The next day, the slides would be sand-covered on Madame's orders.

Yet all were willing to give Madame a hand during the winter. It was a long walk for her from the main school to the portable, even though it was just one long slide away for us. She used to grab two or four kids to help her keep balanced in the black spike-heeled stylish boots she wore during the winter months. We were instructed to hold onto her arms, one person on either side, with one behind and one also in front of her. This way, if she fell, there was bound to be one person who would cushion her fall. It was a very tense scene, as the person behind her was itching to give her a shove, and the person in front was aching with nervousness, knowing full well that the one shove would flatten them! But aside from all the quirky aspects of Madame, she was a gem of a French teacher. She livened up my public school days, and remains among my fondest memories and darkest fears of my elementary school. *Vive la française!*

Wilma Flintstone (pseudonym)

Written by Laily, age 17, before the mighty storm hit.

IT'S AS SIMPLE AS 1-2-3 ... 6!
ELAINE'S METHOD
December 2013

Elaine Groothuysen

Today, through procedural writing, I will be teaching you how to knit a scarf. The same technique can be used for a variety of types of clothing. Let's begin.

MATERIALS: wool thread/yarn of various colours, two knitting needles. Approximately $5 per ball of yarn.

STEP 1: Tie a knot around one of the needles.
STEP 2: Take the other needle and slide it through the backside of the knot.
STEP 3: Loop the thread around the second needle and behind the back of the knot.
STEP 4: Pull the loop with the 2nd needle back out of the knot.
STEP 5: Now pull a new loop around the first needle.
STEP 6: Repeat this procedure over and over again to the desired length.

FINAL NOTE:

Once again, this technique for knitting a scarf can be used for a variety of clothing materials, such as bandanas, head bands, mittens, and Afghan throws. Other knitters may apply different techniques to do their handiwork.

Best of luck with your knitting! Winter's here, so start threading!

SONNET ON LIFE
April 2009

Judy Evans

I am sixty-six years young.
I feel like I am twenty years young.
I want to live a long, happy life,
Without too much strife.
I want to learn something new every day.
I want to love, create, to be generous,
To write, to laugh, to read the newspaper;
To write poetry that is fabulous.
To help, to stay healthy, mentally and physically.
To speak positively.
To hardly ever get angry.
To die in my sleep, then to go to Heaven,
To see family, friends, to be reborn.

**"Faith makes all things possible. Love makes all
things easy."**

Dwight L. Moody

MIRACLE FROM ABOVE
The Mike Martin Story
March 2011

Michael Martin

I was known as Teenage Mike. I was only 17 when the most incredible thing happened to me. To this day, I still can't understand or explain how it happened, but it did. It really did!

I lived with my father in a small town called Beachville. It was named Beachville, rightly so, due to dozens of beaches that ran along the Pacific Ocean. The town was a friendly place, lots of kids, and many fishermen trying to feed their families. My father was also a fisherman and often brought home a variety of large fish and lobster for us to eat. My mother was a retired actress who worked in the movies during the 50's, but had recently passed away from cancer. This devastated my father and me, who were very close to her. We were her only family. Since the death of my mother, Dad and I attempted to live and work together, but it was very difficult.

The weeks and the months passed. Being a fisherman was difficult. My father was not able to bring home enough for our two mouths to eat. For this reason, my dad had to take on another job as foreman of a construction company. This helped him out in supporting our family of two. Actually, our family of three! With the two of us taking care of the house, we had a handy sidekick with us ... we loved him very much. He was a small Cocker Spaniel named Scamp. Scamp was a very friendly dog. I used to enjoy throwing a ball and having him run to retrieve it. He listened very well. He loved when I held the ball up in my right hand. This meant I was ready to play and so was Scamp!

He was a great friend and he made me and my dad very happy. And then, one day …

"Come on, kiddo! We're heading out to sea. You're joining me today!"

I'll never forget those few words he hollered out to me on a blustery day in May. These were words that would ring in my head for a long, long time. Why? Because, on that trip, many years ago, something happened to me, changing my life forever. You might say it "kicked" my life in an entirely different direction. At the time, though, it didn't seem so grand.

The boat revved up and made its way past the docks. It was moving quickly through the water. It was rocking back and forth, and my dad and I nearly fell over. We didn't realize the wind and the waves were so crazy that day, as we continued to go further into the deep water.

"Son, where do you want to head?"

"Wherever the fish are biting, Newsey!" Newsey was a nickname I used for my father. I don't know why!

The waves continued to rock the boat. The wake behind us was very wide, which worried my father. He did not want to lose control of the boat in these foamy, large waves. The two of us zoomed over to a nearby favourite spot to drop our lines.

The boat slowed down and I started to get my fishing rod ready. We stopped and I slipped and fell inside the boat! Dad laughed and said, "Is that a fish, or just you, you clumsy fool! Haha!"

"Pretty funny, Dad!"

I baited the rod and got ready to cast. I swung the rod back, nearly hitting my father, and whipped the fishing line and lure into the air. It landed with a "plop" a distance away. Meanwhile, my dad sat behind me in a chair. He was wearing the fisherman's hat with stupid looking feathers on it that he always wore. I tried to hide it on him once, but Scamp had discovered it. Bad boy!

For the next few minutes, I waited patiently for a bite, but it seemed like nothing was coming.

"Maybe we should go back, Dad. There's nothing here!"

Just as I spoke those words, there was a tug on my line.

"I got a bite! I got a bite!"

I began to yank on the rod and reel the fish in. Then, for some odd reason, I looked up and noticed that the clouds had turned grey, and the wind had picked up. Slowly, as I pulled and pulled on the line, our once sunny day had become a black day in my life.

I fought the fish as it came closer to the boat. It was a big fish and very powerful. Dad helped me with a net to pull it into the boat. It was a fish like we'd never seen before.

"What the heck is that? What kind of fish? I've never seen anything like that! It's HUGE!"

The fish landed THUMP into the boat. It was jumping up and down. I reached down with a glove and tried to prevent it from wiggling. Suddenly, the fish leapt off the bottom of the boat and bit me on the lower part of my leg.

"It hurts! It hurts! Dad! Dad!"

I fell to the bottom of the boat and grabbed my leg. My leg was hurting so much—it was near the kneecap and it was bleeding. My father grabbed the first aid kit and began to bandage my leg. He was like the Good Samaritan. As he did, a large rumble sounded and a flash of lightning struck the sky. Rain started to pour down.

"We better get back to shore quickly, or your leg will never be healed. We got to get you to a hospital!"

Dad started the motor and gunned it through the water as the rain began to come down harder. My leg was really hurting and I grabbed it tightly. The raindrops were hitting my face like little stones. It was hard to see, but dad moved faster and faster to shore.

The boat finally arrived at our dock. My father asked me to hop out of the boat. I stepped one foot into the water and …

"OH! This sucks! Dad, it hurts!"

My dad got up and out of the boat and took me in his arms. We walked over to a nearby bench.

"We got to get you to a hospital! Your leg does not look good!"

We hopped into the car and headed to see the town doctor. The swelling started to go down a bit. We arrived at the hospital. Dad explained what happened and I went into the examining room.

2 HOURS LATER …

"Michael, so sorry about your leg. We have good news and bad news. The good news … you're alive. The bad news is that we've discovered that you have a very rare, special bone in your leg, and it has been damaged. You have a hairline fracture."

"A what?"

"A fracture."

"A who—who's fractured?"

"Mike, you must be hallucinating. You have a crack in a rare bone inside your leg. Come here. Take a look at this x-ray. As you can see, part of this special bone is fractured. I hate to say this, Mike, but unless we send you to a specialist immediately, you may never walk again."

"Uhhh … excuse me? But, Doc! I'm a kid. I have to walk!"

"Yes, and I'm hoping you'll be able to, but we're going to have to fly you down to Colombia."

"Colombia? Where's Colombia?"

I stood up and fell back down.

"Hold your horses, kid! Stay still, will yah? We're going to get you there, but you'll have to go alone. The flight and the work will be too expensive, so your dad will have to stay put here."

"WOO! A week without my dad! But wait ... you mean I'll be alone the whole time?"

"Relax, kid. We'll take care of all of it."

FLIGHT DAY ... TAKEOFF TIME ...

"Man, I'm scared. I hate planes!"

I took my seat on the busy plane. I grabbed some food out of my bag and a metal chain that my dad had given me for strength. I also put on my dad's construction helmet for safety. I looked absolutely ridiculous, but you just never know! I had a scrapbook for drawing cartoons ... and yes, pretty ladies! I love to draw. Love it! You should see my scrapbook!

The plane took flight. It was a bumpy start as I held onto the seat's arms for dear life. It was not easy but, as the plane ascended, I noticed white clouds outside, and I started to feel more relaxed, like I was in Heaven or something. All of a sudden, feeling tired, I dozed off.

A VISIT TO LA LA LAND

I dreamt about my fishing trip with my dad. Only this time, I was the only one fishing. The fishing line started to tug as I drew in a large fish. Surprisingly, it was the same fish that I had caught back home—the exact fish that bit me. Unlike back home with my father, there was something really strange going on ... especially when the fish opened its mouth and said, "Hey, man! I bit you. I know all about it and I want to tell you I meant no harm. I'm a fish. I bite! That's what fish do!"

"What about my leg? That hurt!" I replied.

"I promise I will never bite you again—or anyone. I am very sorry."

"I accept your apology, but I can barely walk now! You should have thought of that before you …"

"Listen, Mike. Because I hurt you so much, this is what I'm going to do for you. Here's a little secret I'm going to throw at you. I have a bad feeling, an omen concerning you and your life. Listen carefully to my words. The surgery you are about to endure will not work out the way you want it to. You will leave the office in Colombia the same as when you got there. You will still be walking, or at least trying to walk, on a broken leg."

"Well, what should I do? I need this leg fixed!" I asked.

"I must go. I will say no more except these three simple words that you must remember. They will change your life: *waves, sand, seashells.*"

"Waves, sand, seashells? What do you mean? Wait, don't go!"

"Waves, sand, seashells … waves, sand, seashells … waves, sand, seashells …"

The plane hit some turbulence and I suddenly woke up from this peculiar dream.

"What a crazy dream! Why did I have that dream? I wonder what it meant. Could this be true? Will the operation really be useless?"

The plane started to descend. I was a bit nervous. The dream was still ringing in my ears … head. It couldn't be right. The doctors would know exactly what to do. It had to have been a nightmare. I have to see them! It's my only hope!

The plane landed and the exit signs lit up. I entered the airport, picked up my luggage, and went to the front doors. Someone with a short navy haircut was waiting with a sign that had my name painted on it: MIKE COME HERE!

"How are you?" the man asked me. "I am here to pick you up and take you to your hotel. I am an employee of your surgeon, Dr. Edwards."

I got into the car and buckled up.

"Welcome to Colombia!"

I took the drive and then hobbled around some of the streets of Colombia. It was very different from back home. I was staying in a cabin near the ocean, but wanted to see a bit of Colombia first. I had never been this far from home.

In my cabin, I put things away. There was a note on the bathroom door:

Dear Michael,

Welcome to Colombia!
We are sorry to hear about your
unfortunate fish bite. We will do
everything to ensure that we fix up
your leg and that you are able to go
back home healthy. We will have a
car here to pick you up at 7 am.
Please pack a bag with you. You
may be with us overnight.

Sincerely,

Dr. Edwards

The rest of the night, I rested nervously in fear of my upcoming operation. I watched TV, read a book (the Bible, hoping for a miracle, of course!) and fell asleep.

Beep, beep, beep … 6:30 am. I woke easily, but was still uneasy about the upcoming procedure. TAP,

TAP, TAP. There was a knock at the cabin door. I grabbed my bag and followed the driver to his car. We were off.

At 8:30, I arrived at the hospital for the surgery. I was brought inside to register at the desk. They then took me to the operating room. The oxygen mask was placed over my face.

"Count down from 10, Michael."

"10, 9, 8, 7, 6, 5, 4 … ZZZZ.…"

The operation lasted almost 7 hours as the surgeon tried to figure out how to fix my bone. At around 4:00 pm, I woke up in the recovery room.

"Welcome back, Michael! We don't have the best news. We could not heal your leg. The problem still persists."

"Oh the trials and tribulations! My gosh! Poor me! Doctor, give me a banana and tell me what I'm going to do!" I said exasperatedly, as I stood up and tried to walk. I could feel bone tissue and I could feel pain.

I returned to the cabin by the ocean. I did not know what to do about my leg. Maybe I would never walk properly again? Maybe I would never walk again? Maybe I'd have to get a cane, or even a wheelchair! This would be difficult for a kid who loved to fish and swim.

I yelled into the sky. "God … why did I go fishing? I should have asked You first! Can You please, somehow, heal my leg? Why me? Why me? What did I do? What should I do?"

Feeling very upset and frustrated, I grabbed a fishing rod and some food, and ran down to the beach where an old, empty, wooden rowboat floated by the shore. I had to get away. I felt like it was calling me to row. I hopped into the boat, grabbed the oars, and started to row out into the calm sea.

I *row, row, rowed the boat* out, but not too far. I placed a worm on my hook and cast the line into the water. After several minutes, there was a tug on the line. I started to reel up but, for some reason, whatever I was pulling up, was pulling down just as hard.

"Where's the darn line? What the heck is down there? Good God!"

For the next 30 minutes, I tugged and tugged on the line, but the fish, or whatever it was, would not cooperate. Suddenly, the line pulled hard, snapping and knocking me right back over the edge of the boat and into the water.

SPLASH!

Treading for my life, I found it very difficult to keep my head above the water. My hurt leg was throbbing with terrible pain. I could barely kick to keep myself up.

I looked up above, trying to find an answer, some kind of help. I did not have enough energy to get into the boat. As I looked up, the sky began to turn dark red and black. Weird. It was only 5:00 pm but, for some reason, the sky was becoming black.

It started to rain, rather heavily; actually, it started to pour. I heard thunder and noticed the sky light up with every boom. It was the worst storm I'd ever seen in my entire life! The water started to move and shift. It began to twirl round and round in a whirlpool fashion. I could barely see anything and yelled up to the clouds.

"God! Please stop this rain! It's driving me bonkers! HELP!"

At that moment, I looked below my feet and noticed a large hole developing. I started to fall deeper and deeper, round and round into the whirling black hole.

"I hope I don't hit bottom! This is crazy!"

I noticed something coming up from the black hole, as my leg continued to hurt. I looked closely at the object as it got bigger and bigger. Was it a shark? Was it a whale? NO! It looked like a girl, but not an ordinary girl. It was a mermaid! A beautiful mermaid, decorated in many glittering colours. She looked at me and said, *"Who's that looking at me?"*

"Can you please tell me who you are? I've been in the water too long. You should be here, but not me! Can you help?"

"Don't you know? I am a mermaid. I can help you if you follow me. This place is very dangerous. It is even unsafe for me. Take my hand."

We made our way toward the black hole.

"Michael, my name is Karen. I am here to help heal your leg. Listen carefully to what I say. You have been through much for a kid. I am here to ensure that your leg works again, and I hope to reunite you with your father. Hold tight."

In what seemed like only a moment, I saw the last number of days flash past my eyes. I looked at my leg and noticed it was still broken. I then watched as the leg started to heal itself right before my eyes! I could not believe it! The pain was floating away. Indeed, a miracle was happening!

Karen spoke up, *"I love you. I always have. I am here because I want you to be happy. I want to make sure you are cared for."*

We both began to cry as I thanked Karen for everything she had done. Another whirlpool began to appear above the two of us in a reverse direction.

"What am I supposed to do now, Karen? I don't want to leave you!"

"I will never leave you. I will always be near you, in your heart and in your soul. Take this and keep it."

She handed me a ring.

"With this magic ring, I may never "see" you again, but I will always be with you, as long as you keep it. This is a special ring, because even though I will never see you again, you will always be in my heart. If you look

through the ring, at any time, you will see no one else except me and the one Who made you."

I took the ring, "You mean everything to me. You saved my life. I will never forget you."

I put the ring on my third finger and immediately started to spin round and round, but this time up, up and up....

"All dreams come true, Michael. It will always be me and you."

My eyes blinked, and then ... POP!

The sun was shining, the water was calm. The birds flew through the air chirping by. I felt the wooden boat around me. My hands were warm and I felt comfortable and secure. I looked across the boat and noticed someone fishing.

"Nothing ... again, Michael! I'll try one last time and then we are out of here! Did you have a nice rest, son? How are you feeling?"

I couldn't understand what was happening. For some reason, I was face to face with my father. Where was I? Just moments ago, I was in Colombia! I remembered everything, my leg, the sea, Karen, the whirlpool. Was everything just a dream?

The only way I could figure out if it was a dream was by feeling for my broken leg. I reached down and rubbed my leg. I moved it around. Nothing. My leg was completely fine! Nothing had happened! It was all a dream ... phew!

I grabbed my rod and stood up. I cast far into the blue.

"What a wild dream!" I exclaimed. "What happened? I can't understand why that dream felt so real." *All dreams come true*, I laughed to myself, *it will always be me and you.* Shyah, right!

And that's when the strangest thing in the world happened. It was truly unbelievable, and it blew my mind. I looked down at my hand. On my third finger, there rested a round steel ring with three words inscribed on it: *waves, sand, seashells.*

HOME SWEET HOME
May 2008

Judy Evans

I live at the Royal Ottawa Place,
Where everyone knows my face,
Since 2004.
I have to be creative to write poetry,
Until the day I die.
I have to live each day as it comes,
Summer, spring, fall, winter, one day at a time.
And remember, as each day passes,
This is the first day of the rest of your life.
I hope and pray to live long,
I have family that loves me,
I have a boyfriend I love,
I hope to remain calm, content, happy.

ROYAL OTTAWA PLACE
Est. 2004

"Home is not where you live, but where they understand you."

Christian Morgenstern

PART IV

INTRIGUE AND IMAGINATION

"A dream you dream alone is only a dream. A dream you dream together is reality."

Yoko Ono

A CHRISTMAS ELEVATOR
September 2014

Sue Racine

I want an elevator for Christmas.
One that has a hot tub,
So I can rub-a-dub-dub,
Whilst I drink my root beer,
Underneath a crystal chandelier.
I want one with a petting zoo,
With at least one kangaroo.
And it would have a small
Country and Western dancehall
For the Petting Zoo Ball.

The elevator would be beside my bed,
So I can get my ups and downs.
(And meet a guy named Fred)
One where I can come and go
Both on the diagonal and sideways,
With a pulley system of rubber hose,
So that no one knows where it goes.
Only I and the petting zoo will know …
And off to the wild blue yonder,
I and the zoo will go!

MY SOUL REJOICE
June 2009

Judy Evans

The teen I met a week ago;
He rumbled on the pad.
He left me with a lost ego,
And cut out all my glad.
And now my days are deep and dark.
My sorrows know no end.
I need a lifting clinging cigarette spark,
And greenbacks for to spend.
And when the joint is dark and low,
And nothing moves with voice,
Music will issue soft and slow,
And make my soul rejoice.

CYCLE OF THE VAMPIRE
Soft, Cuddly & Bloodily
October 2011

Daniel Parent

John Mays was head custodian at the Cinema Square on Queen Street in Ottawa. The Square was not your ordinary movie theatre, and not always a friendly place to hang around. But it was a very popular theatre in town, since the early 1900's. Especially on a Friday night, October 30th to be exact, at 4:00 pm, where anything could and would happen. With its dark paint, high ceilings, and gothic look, it was the perfect place to watch a flick, with or without a date.

The Square was owned and run by a kind, intelligent man, well respected by his workers and the general public. Although his standards were high, and there was a high turnover of workers, he never had to worry about John. John just went about doing his own business, day after day, night after night. For some reason, John didn't worry about his job as custodian. What John didn't know was that he possessed a condition deep inside of him that no one knew about.

From the young age of nineteen, John had had a keen fascination with bats. He didn't know why, but he found them so interesting, wild and weary, always on the run, or should we say, the fly! Over the next dozens of years, John had a strange habit of hunting and collecting bats of all kinds, without knowing the real reasons why they followed him around. He never knew that he was using mind tricks to lure them in, to make them his own. He thought they just liked being around him. It was scary, a bit frightening, but John seemed to love them all, big and small.

As John grew into a man, and reached his 64th birthday, two big things happened in his life. First off, he was hired as the new head custodian at the theatre, which he was thrilled about. The second, he was not too thrilled about. Something strange started to happen to his body, something he could not understand or control. For some reason, he noticed that, at certain times of the day, his skin looked shiny and felt smoother and warmer than normal. Closer to sundown, he sometimes felt like he was having a heart attack or a nervous breakdown, because his heart was pounding so quickly in his chest, feeling like it just wanted to pop out! He didn't know why this was happening. On so many nights, he ended up popping two Tylenol into his body. That seemed to calm his nerves for a time, but he started to wonder what the heck was happening to him. He would find out very soon …

It was around five o'clock on that Friday evening, one day before Halloween. The theatre was extremely busy as people crowded into their seats for the main attraction of the weekend. The theatre was premiering its showing of the horror classic, *Dracula*. Everyone was scared, but also eager to see this classic piece that was being shown all over town. Rumours of the excitement created a buzz in the city.

John adjusted his name tag, closed the theatre doors, and walked behind the large movie screen in the old-fashioned theatre. With a tug of a rope, the curtains slowly opened and the crowd began to tremble as the eerie music started to play.

John returned to the lobby to do his cleaning. The hours ticked away until it was 9:00 pm. Since it was a theatre that closed early, people from the second showing started to file out, weaving and bobbing through the lobby. This was always John's least favourite time of night, the long and boring theatre clean-up time, ugh. He never knew what he'd find. And the worst was the gum, the dreaded gum! It wouldn't be too bad tonight, since not many kids were old enough to watch *Dracula*.

Phew! He always wondered why his boss put that stupid gum ball machine in the lobby. It was John's worst nightmare!

Or was it?

As the last few moviegoers exited, John locked the building's doors and did his final clean up in the theatre, what he called "the polishing act". He was a proud man and a hard worker. He always did a bang-up job. He worked for a while, finished up, and put his mop and broom into storage. His job for the night was done … for now.

"Phew, good to be done for the day. What a busy crowd!" he said, as he found a ten dollar bill underneath a bench in the lobby. "Wow! I'm rich!" he laughed. He was happy with his finding as he whipped his coat on and buttoned up for October's fall breeze. He locked the front glass doors and stepped out into the cool wind. Brrrr.

On his way home, heading toward downtown, John started to feel his heart acting up again, as it did every night around this same time. But, for some strange reason, though it occurred each evening for a while now, he seemed to forget that it ever happened to him before. Each night, it was like he was experiencing this strange phenomenon for the very first time.

"Oh, God! I'm alone and my heart is pounding. I wish I had someone to share my problem with!" He thought he was having what he called, a "nineteenth nervous breakdown", or maybe even a heart attack! He raced through the streets, practically knocking people over.

"Hey, watch where you're going, you jerk!" some man hollered from his car, as John dodged across the street. He didn't seem to care whatsoever. He was in big trouble and he knew it. Was he dying? He became very concerned and would not let anything stand in his way. Up ahead, he noticed a Convenience 'R' Us

Pharmacy. Approaching the door, he realized that, for some odd reason, the 24-hour store was closed. Convenient! "Darn! Curses! Foiled again! I'm dying here!" he cried out, looking kind of foolish, since no one was around him. John grabbed his chest and gave it a good pounding, punching into it like King Kong doing a beat down.

"Ahhhh!" he yelled, at the top of his lungs.

Thank goodness, he then felt something in his side coat pocket. He pulled out a lifesaving bottle of Tylenol and quickly swallowed down a few. This seemed to numb the pain, and he continued toward home.

He finally arrived home around 11:30 pm. It was late and his walk took a lot longer because of his condition. He entered his dark habitat, a place he had recently moved into. He was not a rich man, but wasn't poor. He could afford a home but, for some odd reason, he preferred to live in a hidden cave on the south side of Ottawa. It was located beside an old, decrepit cemetery, no longer being used.

He entered the cave and staggered along the wall, using it to hold himself up. His heart continued to throb feverishly, and he fell face first onto the cement ground. His face hit the floor hard, leaving a large gash in his forehead. That'll hurt tomorrow, he said to himself, as small drips of blood made their way to the ground. And then suddenly … IT … began.

He looked at his right arm and noticed that it was disappearing and reappearing right before his eyes. Was he imagining this? Was this for real? He grabbed the pill bottle, squinted, and looked at the label. "Tylenol" it read, of course. Then he noticed his skin becoming very shiny. In only seconds, it looked as though it was starting to rot before his eyes. It also started to turn black as blisters appeared all over his body.

He tore off his shirt and blood continued to drip down from his forehead. One by one, suddenly his limbs deteriorated right before him. He could see all around him but he could no longer see his body, his heart … maybe his soul?

"AHG! Curses! What's happening to me? Am I losing my mind? Good God!" he hollered, his words echoing in the cave.

And then, without warning, to the right and left of him, wings began to form and poke out from a body that he could not even see! But he could definitely feel the wings! They felt sticky and slimy as they started to flap, and then he noticed something else. It actually felt amazing!

"Oh my Gaaa!" he screamed, as his body started to rise up from the floor.

"Dagnabbit! What the heck is happening here?" John snickered, using his comical Bugs Bunny voice. Rising up in the air gave him SUCH a high, he just felt like laughing!

"WOOO!" As the wings continued to rise up and down, John rose higher and higher in his secret cavern. From now on, maybe he'd have to call it his "bat cave"? Gheesh! He looked way down and moved his head from side to side. He could see the pictures of people and animals on the walls below him. From way up there, things looked very different. He noted how small his couch looked, until he ended up bumping his head on the rock ceiling.

"I guess I won't be needing that couch anymore," he joked. "Maybe I'll need to carry a freakin' sleeping bag! This is nuts! This is ridiculous! What in God's name is going on?"

John couldn't believe it! This was so absurd! This was monumental for him, although, without remembering, the same thing had happened dozens of times already over the last year. He just had no recollection of it. But now that it had happened … he LOVED it! Where would he go? He could freakin' fly darnit! What in the world would he do? The world was now his friend and he knew it was time to explore … I'VE GOT THE POWER!

> *"It's gettin', it's gettin', it's gettin' kinda hectic.*
> *It's gettin', it's gettin', it's gettin' kinda hectic."*

With *SNAP*'s "The Power" ringing through his head, he started to put on a groove as he felt his way around his cozy confines. He dropped down and grabbed some tomato juice out of the fridge (or was it tomato juice?) and a chewy, fruity coconut. He nibbled away on it and downed some juice, and then … HE FLEW BABY, FLEW!

John flew through the downtown area. He looked below and everything looked so normal, but so small. The people looked small, the cars and buses looked small, and even the boats near the marina looked small. Everything was so freakin' tiny!

"This is strange yet so wild at the same time! What the heck is going on? I love it, but … I'm losing my mind!"

His wings flapped and flapped as he headed toward a familiar place. He seemed to know exactly where he was going. It looked like he was heading out of the city and into the forest. The lights of the city started to fade away as he hit the outskirts. He could see the bright moon and the stars, but the city lights were no longer visible. For once, he was free from the stress and hassles of his life. All of that was left behind as he descended into an open area between several tall trees. Finally, he landed on the branch of a large maple tree. His wings halted and he rested.

"Phew! Jeepers, creepers, it's SO weird being a bat. I'll have to get used to this. I wonder if I'll ever be a person again!" he said, as he looked to the east and looked to the west.

He decided to fly around the forest to see all that he could see. Below, he saw many trees, some patches of grass, several different flowers, and a stream curving its way among the trees. He flew up above the tallest of trees. The stars were glittering in the dark evening sky.

"Hmm … I'm getting a bit tired and a bit hungry. It is time to find me some delicious food. Where are the burgers, man?" he said to himself, but quickly realized that wouldn't do. He made his way down to the creek below, landing on a small stone in front of the water.

"Slurp, slurp …"

John took a sip of the cool water. It did not satisfy him. Next, he found a frog along the bank of the creek. He licked the frog. Yuck! It was disgusting! Then, he found a squirrel that was lying in a pile of colourful leaves. It was not moving. It was dead. John took a bite with his new, sharp white fangs, but, guess what? Even that didn't satisfy his hunger! He was hungry for more. There was something missing in these delicious foods (yah, right!). The water didn't do it, the frog was no good, and neither was the squirrel.

John wanted more … so much more!

"Dagnabbit! This is awful! I'm SO hungry, but what can I eat? What will I do to satisfy my hunger?"

John flew up and searched for food everywhere. Finally, he stumbled upon a hidden graveyard embedded deep within the confines of the forest. He swooped down to the ground and started to look at all the gravestones planted in the moist grass. He wondered if there was any food there. Suddenly, he experienced the biggest shock … no wait … the biggest scare he'd ever felt in his entire life! Standing tall in front of him was a cement gravestone shaped like a cross.

Interesting, he thought, as he looked carefully at the words inscribed in the stone:

John Mays
RIP – October 30, 1956

"NOOOOO! How could this be? How could I be down there, when I'm right here? How can this be possible? How can this be true? What in God's name is going on? Is someone playing games with me?" John had an abundance of questions, of course! He couldn't believe it. He was actually staring at his own grave! He didn't know what to do next, so he walked around the gravestone a couple of times and then flew up to a tree high above to meditate on this revelation. As he hung from the tree branch, he started to think about everything that had happened to him that night:

1. His name was John.
2. He was not normal at all.
3. He could turn into a bat ... what?
4. He was as hungry as a starving dog!

Number 4 seemed to matter most. He needed to find food NOW! But what did bats eat? Hmmm?

Off he flew in search of food, but he had no clue what he wanted, so instead, he just flew and flew and flew aimlessly in the dark night.

He made it to the other edge of the forest and headed toward another part of the city. The streets were clear and the moon kept shining brightly. He began to look below for a place to land, to eat, to sleep. All of a sudden, he noticed a small red brick building in the middle of an empty parking lot.

"This looks like an interesting place to land. Maybe I can find some food and get some rest." He flew down to the glass doors and stuck onto the window, wings spread out.

"Great! Now what?" he said to himself. "I just need to get in. Hello? Someone? Anyone?"

In the hallway, a gentleman was sweeping the lobby. For some reason, the man looked over and noticed the bat stuck on the window. John saw him approach. Finally, he was going to get in. The door opened slowly and, instead of a nice welcome inside, the custodian took his broom and banged on the glass, knocking John right off!

"Ahhhh!" Thud!

John landed on his left wing with a big bump, as the custodian walked away. Feeling lousy and still tired, John rolled over onto his back and lay on the grass. He was very sleepy. In only a few minutes, beside a comfy courtyard, he fell asleep.

THE NEXT MORNING ...

John rolled over and looked all around him.

"Where am I?" He had a bad headache as he looked around. He was lying on the wet grass and in front of him was a red brick building. He looked down at himself. He was no longer a bat lying on the grass. He was a human being—he was back to being John again, clothes and all! He seemed to have no memory of the craziness from the night before. The theatre, the cave, the forest, the graveyard ... he couldn't remember any of it, including who he was! Everything had seemed to fade away ... FOR NOW.

John got back onto his feet, which felt really weird. He dusted himself off and looked up at the early morning sun. Quickly, he turned his head from the light, avoiding the brightness. It was far too bright for his eyes and he could feel them burning, literally. He quickly threw the hood of his sweater over his head to protect himself from the light.   He walked over to the glass door, forgetting completely that he was stuck to it the night before! Beside the window was a sign that read:

ROYAL OTTAWA PLACE
Est. 2004

"Where am I? Where could I be? Have I lost it? Who am I?"

John started to panic, wondering who he was and how he ended up landing in front of this strange building. He reached into his pocket for something, anything that would help him to remember who he was. He pulled out a handful of change and a ten dollar bill. Then he felt a card in his pocket. He pulled the card out and took a look. It was an ID card that had his name on it.

JOHN MAYS
HEAD CUSTODIAN

"This sounds familiar—I kinda remember being a custodian sometime, but what am I doing here? I don't recognize this place at all!"

John entered the building. As he walked into the front lobby, he was greeted kindly by a man who shook his hand and smiled, "How are you? My name is Dan. Dan Parent."

"Nice to meet you, Dan. I'm ..." he glanced quickly at his card and looked back up, "John Mays."

The two of them looked strangely at each other. It was like they knew each other from the past: a faraway past. Danny brought John to the front desk.

"John, you can speak to this nurse." Danny waved goodbye ... for now. "How can I help you, sir?" the head nurse asked politely.

Dazed and confused as to who he was and what he was doing at this odd building, he looked at his card again and said, "Here." He handed the nurse his ID and she looked at it, scratching her head. Bothered and bewildered, she said, "Uh ... I guess ... you must be the new head custodian. Finally our prayers have been answered! We have been without one for some time now."

"Uh … yah … I guess," John replied.

"Everyone, this is John, our new head custodian."

"Hello there … Welcome, John … Nice to meet you, John!"

Everyone seemed so nice. And with that, John found out, not only who he was, but why he was here. He finally felt some relief.

John familiarized himself with the building. He found out that ROP was a residence in the heart of Ottawa that housed approximately a hundred people, all of whom had lived there because of different mental and physical ailments.

It was a three-floored building with two wings of rooms on each floor. John was mainly responsible for the second and third floors. Duties would include washing floors, cleaning rooms and yes, his favourite … the washrooms. Yuck!

Throughout the day, John worked hard to make sure he got the job done and done well. He noticed he was a neat freak. He always made sure his job was done immaculately.

In the afternoon, John entered a room on the third floor with his broom. Lying on the bed, listening to the radio, as he always did, was Danny. Danny had lived at ROP for a while.

"Hello … Danny, right?"

"How are you … John, right?"

"Yes, that's right. What are you doing?"

"What does it look like I'm doing? Haha!"

"Yah, I guess that was a stupid question. I should have asked, what are you listening to?"

"Music, news, different stuff."

"Who's your favourite band?"

"*The Beatles*, of course!"

"Love *The Beatles*. Do you want to hold my hand?"

"Help!" Danny sang out. "I need somebody!"

"I'm kidding, Dan, I'm kidding!"

"So am I, but they are a great band—classic."

After a bit of chit-chat, Danny got up off the bed and stepped into the washroom and locked the door behind him. CLICK! He usually never locked this door.

John began to sweep away, even under the bed. There was not much to sweep up. Dan kept his room very clean, tidier than a bottle of Mr. Clean. As he moved along, trying to find something dirty, he felt a sudden ache in his chest. His heart started to beat feverishly and his head began to sweat. It felt swollen suddenly. He then felt a strong urge for something, a need for something. But what was it?

CLICK! CLICK! CLICK! Dan was having some trouble getting the lock open. Was the lock telling him something? Finally, he got it open and came out. John was standing there. Dan looked suspiciously at John, and John looked suspiciously at Dan. John didn't look so good.

"Oh, man, are you okay? Maybe you should sit down."

The two of them sat on the bed. Danny grabbed a facecloth for John so he could wipe his forehead. Danny asked again, "Are you feeling okay?" He looked concerned. John sat there, but he would not say another word. He was quiet, almost transfixed on the clock on the wall. He seemed to be in a trance. An urge for something was building, but he didn't know what.

Then, he eventually figured it out. He needed it and needed it right NOW! It was blood! He needed blood! John finally came to grips with the reality that he was NOT a custodian. He was NOT a man. He was NOT an animal. No, even worse. He was a CREATURE OF THE NIGHT!

He could feel something happening in his mouth. Out of the blue, his teeth started to grow long and sharp.

He could feel them with his tongue, and actually cut his tongue causing it to bleed. Then, with one leap, he flew into the air and pounced on top of Danny.

Dan screamed, "Help! Somebody get me outta here!"

But it was too late. John had already bit down on Danny's neck. Delicious, John thought, as he started to mumble and lick his lips. Blood ran down the side of his mouth.

Danny stood up and then sat back down on his bed. He was dazed and confused and it seemed like he didn't remember anything. His eyes were rolling in his head and his eyelids were blinking rapidly. John stood by the window watching, continuing to lick his lips. He watched as Danny's eyes started to swell and water. He could only see the whites of Danny's eyes as he rocked slowly back and forth on the bed. And, as the clock ticked on the wall, with every passing second, Danny's eyes began to close until he finally passed out. He fell off the bed and onto the floor. THUMP.

John didn't realize, as he hovered over Danny, that he was no longer the same person. He was no longer a vampire. The curse had evaporated into the air. He was free and, mysteriously, remembered nothing. But what about Danny?

John ran into the hall to look for someone to help. He hollered down the hallway, "Somebody, help! It's Danny!"

Another custodian, Tim, the broom guy, ran into the room, as did two nurses who followed. They got Danny onto the bed and covered his body. He was shivering and his skin was pale and cold. John stood back by the window. He was speechless and in shock.

"Danny, Danny, you okay?" Tim asked, as he made monkey faces and tickled his toes. Danny started to laugh and his eyes opened. Miraculously, in only minutes, his skin started to warm up and the colour in his face returned to normal.

"Phew!" Tim exclaimed. "Welcome back, Danny!"

John, who started to finish up his sweeping, was moving around like nothing had even happened.

The hours passed and Danny lay on his bed, listening to his Walkman as usual. He seemed fine, back to normal. At around 7:30 pm, the nurses got ready for their evening shifts. Nancy grabbed her tray and headed down the hall. She made a few stops and then arrived at Danny's room.

"Hi, how are you feeling, Danny? Are you okay? Can I come in?"

Not a word was spoken.

"Would you like something? Are you hungry?"

Still, there was no noise … at all. The nurse called in one more time and nervously tiptoed into the room. Surprisingly, Danny was not in his room! His bed was made, and there was an imprint of his body on the comforter, but no Danny!

She ran down the hall to the nurses' station.

"Has anyone seen Danny? He's always in his room at this time. Where could he be?"

"Oh, he's probably in the washroom."

"No, I checked … it's empty!"

"Did you check the television room?"

She ran into the lounge, but all she saw were Barry and Randy watching television. Barry was practically asleep on one of the couches.

"Boys! Have you seen Danny? We can't seem to find him!"

They grunted and growled. They had not seen him since dinner. The nurse ran down the hall calling out Danny's name! She was in a complete state of shock. She called down to the first floor. Nothing. Suddenly, the hallway alarms started to ring as residents started to pop their heads out of their rooms. The intercom called out aloud, "Would Danny please report to the nurses' station immediately!"

Time passed quickly and 9:00 pm came. The search had lasted a long while and they had come up with nothing. Danny was nowhere in sight. The nurses and workers were baffled. This had never happened before. Nurses continued to search well into the night, while police were called on an emergency run.

"When did you last see Daniel?"

One of the social workers spoke up, "Please, you have to find him. He's never left the building on his own before. We just can't understand it. I'm very confused. He loves it here!"

All night, they searched the building and surrounding grounds. The search, the police told them, would continue. They would find him. They would find him, or his body.

A WEEK LATER …

There was a rap at the door of the Cinema Square theatre.

TAP, TAP, TAP …

A balding man opened the door and greeted a gentleman wearing only black (pants, shirt, sports jacket). The two men shook hands.

"I'm applying for your head custodian position."

"Yes, welcome. I'm the owner. Come on in."

The man was hired right on the spot. It was as though the owner knew him from somewhere. The owner told him that his former custodian just seemed to vanish into thin air. "We've been searching for a week now. He was a great worker. This theatre became a ghost town once rumours started to fly concerning his disappearance. When can you start?"

"Right away." The sign for a new custodian was taken down. It had only been posted up an hour before. It was surprising how quickly the mysterious man had shown up for the job, almost as though it was planned. It was also timed perfectly, kind of like it was meant to happen ... and so it did.

"Oops," the owner scratched his head, "I forgot to ask. What is your name, sir?"

"Danny," was all the man ever said. The owner never asked more. His life and everything about him would remain a mystery ... for a time.

ONE YEAR LATER ...

It was 4:00 pm on a Friday night, October 30th. Dan, head custodian of the Cinema Square, was sweeping the floor getting ready for a 5 pm show. Since it was close to Halloween, the theatre was presenting its annual Halloween showing of the horror classic, *Dracula*. It would be a scary evening for the big crowd that would settle in for a shaker, a screamer, and a hair-pulling experience. It was a movie like no other!

Danny opened the doors to a long lineup down the street. People started to tumble into the theatre, awaiting the highly anticipated start of the movie. Danny started his sweeping and cleaning of the lobby even before the movie started. It got messy that quickly. He reached into his shirt pocket and pulled out a Mars Bar, his favourite. He walked into his little office once he was finished. The big rush of work would come following the show. For now, he made some coffee, sat back in his chair and took a sip. Slowly, his eyes got tired. He would rest, but only for a short time.

9:00 PM

The last of the moviegoers made their way home as Danny locked the glass doors. On his way out, he turned off the lights and stepped into the street. Moments later, something happened. His heart started to pound quickly in his chest.

"I got to sit down. Man, I feel dizzy. What's going on here? I don't feel so hot."

Danny found a park bench near a parking lot. His heart was nearly jumping out of his skin. He reached into his pocket.

"What's this?"

He pulled out a bottle of Tylenol and popped in a few.

"Ahh … much better." It worked instantly.

He sat on the bench and looked up at the moon. It was full tonight.

And so, that night, for the first time in a year, Danny, like his predecessor, John, would transform into a bat and fly into the dark night, never to return to the theatre again.

THE NEXT DAY …

One year to the date he went missing, a familiar face would arrive back at ROP, naked, lying on the front lawn. He looked different, his face hidden behind a bushy beard, his skin, old and decrepit, and his eyes dark, deep and profound. He would be found by one of the workers and brought into the office, blanket on shoulders.

"Danny's back!"

Although everyone was relieved to have him back, he returned a changed man. On the outside, he looked the same, minus the beard, of course. But on the inside, he was a little strange, a little different. His absence over the year was diagnosed as a memory lapse. He was accepted wholeheartedly by everyone in the residence. Why? They knew him, they loved him, and he was one of them ... or was he?

And so, the next custodian, another new one, would be hired at the theatre, again, and the cycle of the vampire would carry on every year ... forever? The cycle would repeat itself, and never would the cross-shaped gravestone in the forlorn forest bear the same name again. The curse would never be lifted unless the head vampire was found and destroyed. To this day, he has never been found. Who would be the next person to continue the cycle of the vampire?

But who was he, the head vampire? Would he ever be found? Would he ever show his face? Those were the questions. To this day, he remains a mystery. Besides, how could anyone ever point a finger at a pleasant, quiet man, who kept to himself and never raised a stink, and was so welcoming to his customers? How could anyone ever suspect a man who had run a successful Ottawa business for God-knows-how-long? And seriously, would you ever think that a simple, elderly man, who ran an old, rickety downtown theatre, could ever be ... *Head Vampire*?

And for these exact reasons, the cycle of the vampire would live on. For how long, no one knew. Up to, and after this day, the head vampire would continue to remain an enigma, never to be known, hunted, or found.

Would his secret ever be stumbled upon? Could you be his next victim? Hopefully not, but remember that not all mysterious things happen on the tall theatre screen. Beware.

A few words of advice ... from now on, keep your collar up!

ANYBODY HOME?
November 2012

David Mallett

November 19, 2012

Dear Mr. and Mrs. Gruesome,

My name is Paul Weirdman and I live in a house across the street from you. Each day, as I sit and have my breakfast, lunch, or dinner, I look across the street and wonder to myself, what do you do in a house that large with blinds on every window? I wonder if you have a seance in there each night, or if you have a sick child inside that you are trying to hide.

Every time I look across the street, I wonder why you have the blinds shut so tightly—no light can escape. What is going on? Night and day, summer or winter, your blinds are closed! Are you a happy family or a depressed one? This just isn't normal! For 6 years, I've been thinking that maybe, just maybe, you have hidden a child in your upstairs room that you don't want anyone to know about. Hmmm?

Are you friendly people or kind of strange? I just want to know. How private can you get? Most people open their blinds and say hello or wave. The least you could do is keep them open some of the time. It is a weird enough block of houses as it is, without having all your blinds closed up. Who are you hiding? What are you hiding?

I remember hearing that, several decades ago, there was an old gentleman who lived in your place in the early 1900s, who shovelled the snow like he was a madman. He would shovel quickly and then head back inside. Was he a butler? Who was this man? Was he an ancestor of yours?

It is all very strange. One day, I actually saw a woman arrive at your door, and the door was slammed right in her face! Can you tell me why you are doing all of these peculiar things? And why is your garage always closed up the way it is? Do you have a butler living in there? Are you renting out your garage? And didn't I see a dish of vomit on your front step one day? Man, this is all too weird!

Where is your dining room? Is it right above the garage? I lived in Orleans for a while, and your house looks similar. Do you have to go upstairs to go to bed? Or, do you sleep downstairs in the living room? Maybe it is at the back? Or, maybe you sleep in the dark musty basement with the big crawling spiders. If so, I wonder, is your basement finished?

Anyway, I was wondering if you can answer some of these questions. This house must be well over one hundred years old. You must hear spirits knocking on the walls all night long. Even before you moved in, there were some other strange people inside. I hear that one of the men back then, the one who purchased the house in the early 1900s, used to stand on his porch and snarl and growl at the kids going by. I also heard a rumour that he died in the basement of the house. There could be a spirit in that house that might not be happy. This gentleman used to howl from the window to scare the children away. It caused many people to move out of the neighbourhood. His name, as I researched, was Mr. James Houndog.

I am simply writing to ask you some of my questions in an appropriate manner. If you can please drop off a letter to me, Paul Weirdman, at 1300 Strange Avenue, it would be greatly appreciated. Then … simply walk away.

Do not ask for me. Just leave, please. It will be best for both of us. Thank you.

Sincerely yours,

Paul Weirdman

P.S. Please do not call the police concerning this letter. This is not a threat. I just want to know the answers to some of my questions. I guess the biggest reason I want answers is that I find it hard to sleep well at night with this one unsettling thought in my mind. As I stare out my window watching you, day after day, I wonder … are you also watching ME?

Chris Nihmey

SOON
March 1997

Laily Kant

Morning.
Clanging alarm.
Too early to rise.
But too tardy to think about it.

Odours.
Burnt toast.
Better skip breakfast, too.
Have to get organized.
Soon.
Real soon.
Tomorrow … maybe.

FRANKENSTEIN: DESCRIPTIVE WRITING
March 2012

Daniel Parent & Chris Nihmey

"THE SCREWBALL" MONSTER

WHO WAS HE?

The name "Frankenstein" was actually the real name of the doctor who created the "monster". His name was Dr. Victor Frankenstein. He came up with an idea to build and create a monster, a mad creature that would keep him company. His idea was a first of its kind but, in the end, his project ended up backfiring on him.

WHOM DID HE CREATE?

The monster he created stood eight feet tall. He was labelled a wretch, with dead, sleepy eyes that stared right through his victims. His skin was filled with rusty sores, the colours of green and grey. He had the bullish strength of ten men and wasn't afraid to use it. Victor had hoped that his creation would be beautiful. Instead, he ended up with a hideous monster.

HOW AND FOR WHAT PURPOSE WAS HE CREATED?

Dr. Frankenstein wanted to make an everlasting artificial life-form that would live on past his days. His experiment, although very smart and clever, ended up failing, becoming a catastrophe when the monster let loose on the world. Victor, who had feared "what the beast had become", fled into the night leaving the monster to roam and prey. The monster spent much time on his own, walking and wandering, searching and running. After some time, the monster finally ran into his creator, demanding that Victor create a female companion for him. Although Victor contemplated this, visions of an entire race of monsters kept him from creating a counterpart. He decided to avoid the project and spent much time trying to get rid of any parts or ideas for the new monster. The monster realized this and got angry, taking his anger out on Victor's wife, Elizabeth, terrorizing and eventually killing her. From that day forward, Victor swore he would search the world over for the monster to destroy him.

WHERE AND WHEN WAS THE STORY CREATED?

The story of Frankenstein was written by Mary Shelley in the United Kingdom (London) in 1818. Shelley was twenty-one when her story was published by a London publishing house. She actually took the story from a dream she'd had. Surprisingly, she started writing her story as part of a competition with three other writers. Who would write the best horror story?

WORLD TRADE CENTER ATTACKS: DESCRIPTIVE WRITING
March 2012

Daniel Parent & Chris Nihmey

CRASH LANDING

WHERE, WHEN and WHAT?

On Tuesday, September 11, 2001 (9/11), between the hours of 8:46 am and 10:28 am, the World Trade Center (North and South Towers) was struck by passenger jets that crashed into each tower, both planes carrying over 300 people. The planes had been hijacked by Al-Qaeda suicide terrorists, whose main objective was to demolish the twin 110-storey structures, both representing the main trading centres of the US. The catastrophe brought both towers down, collapsing under their own weight, and plunging to the ground below. This sacred area was subsequently named *Ground Zero*.

Two other jet airliners were also hijacked the same morning. One plane ended up crashing into the US Pentagon, the other in a field in Pennsylvania. The latter had been redirected from its original course due to the valiant efforts of its passengers who intervened to try to stop the hijackers' evil intentions. It was intended to hit the White House, home of the President.

WHO?

The attacks that day were devastating. The buildings' demise brought tears and sadness to a city that had always stood confident and powerful, the "city that never sleeps". It would no longer be, as thousands would perish in the attack. Who would plan and coordinate an event of such catastrophic proportions?

His name was Osama Bin Laden, head of the Islamic terrorist group, Al-Qaeda. He would engineer an act like no other, a destructive message to the United States, and one that nobody saw coming. This included President George W. Bush, who was visiting an elementary school early that morning. To his dismay, he was notified of the horrific incident while reading to a class of children!

WHY?

The September 11th attacks on the World Trade Center happened for several reasons, one being that Al-Qaeda wished to severely disrupt the economy of the Western world. It also wanted to expose the vulnerability of the United States to armed attack. At the same time, it would spread fear throughout the United States. A war on terrorism would not only start then, but would continue indefinitely. Power and money have always controlled our world. This is a perfect example of the destruction that both bring to the fight for world domination.

HOW WILL THEY RECOVER?

How do you ever recover as a nation from the horrific loss of over 3,000 innocent lives, people who did not deserve to die? How do you comfort and console the thousands of children who lost parents, left covered in the rubble below? How do well over 6,000 victims recover, who have to live with the nightmares that demolished their country, their nation, their families, and their safety and security? And although emergency workers (firefighters, doctors, paramedics and police officers, etc.) made every effort to save lives, the dark

Reflections From Another Side

and smoky memories of the towers collapsing will never fade. They can never forget. They now hope and pray for better days.

135

MURDER ON LAKE LOUISIANA
October 2013

Sue Racine

It was Wednesday morning, April 18, 1996. Wendy Redfield was taking a nice morning jog down by the river. The air was chilly but comfortable. She wore a light blue shirt with black pants. She often wore these for her early morning exercise. While jogging, she noticed someone coming toward her. It was her friend Frank. They greeted each other with a hug and a kiss on the cheek.

"Good morning. Did you sleep well?" Frank asked. "You look tired."

"Well, actually, I didn't sleep very well because someone was knocking on my door, at 5:30! It startled me."

Frank interrupted, "Who was it?"

"Not sure," replied Wendy. "It is really strange though. Who goes knocking on a door at five in the morning? Anyway, will you join me for breakfast? My treat."

"Definitely!"

Frank walked back with Wendy to her large cabin located on top of a grassy hill. Approaching the house, it started to rain—and boy, did it pour!

They managed to get inside safely. When they entered the kitchen, they noticed that many cupboard doors were opened, and items of food were missing. Frank walked over to the fireplace. It was ablaze. Someone had been in the house! Frank went into the washroom.

Wendy walked into the bedroom of her loft and noticed clothing laid out on the bed.

"Oh my goodness, where did these come from?"

She leafed through a pile of men's clothing. "Strange," she said to herself. Inside the washroom, Frank noticed something very odd as well. He noticed that there were children's toys lying on the bathroom floor.

"Hey, Wendy! What are these toys doing in here? Your daughters are too old for baby toys!"

"What? What toys?"

Wendy put her hand on her forehead. What in God's name was going on? She started to feel disoriented as she pieced the strange happenings together in her head. She had left her home in the early morning. She lived alone, and her daughters were too old for toys. What the heck were toys doing in her house? Something was not right. Somebody had been in her home!

So many questions ran through her mind. What did Frank know about this strange happening? Why had she conveniently met up with him on her run near the water? She was having feelings that were hitting way too close to home. Years of bickering, arguments, and fighting, along with mental stress and a father her children barely saw, were enough to bring back all the uneasy feelings. What the heck were men's clothes doing on her bed? Had her ex made a surprise visit? She was very confused. He hadn't been in this house for at least a month now.

"Alright, Frank, we better forget breakfast."

"But, Wendy, I don't want to leave you like this, alone."

She reassured Frank that she'd be fine. He gave her a hug and headed down toward the river.

RRRRRING!

A phone call caught Wendy by surprise. She picked up the bedroom telephone.

"Hello?"

"Hello." It was a muffled voice. "I know all about you."

Wendy swallowed and breathed nervously. Her heart began to pound.

"Who is this? John, is that you?" she asked, wondering if her brother was playing a trick on her again.

"Where have you been?" the man asked.

"What's it to you? Why are you calling, John? You know I hate these games!"

"This is not John, and this is not a game."

"What do you want? Who is this, really?" Wendy urged. She was now starting to panic as she paced around the room.

"Have you looked at the photo by your bedside lately? Maybe you should have a little peep. Just a little one...." The voice trailed on with a cough and heavy breathing.

Wendy scratched her head. "Why are you asking and how do you know about the picture?" Only her daughters knew about that picture.

"Go find it ... NOW!" the disgruntled voice demanded.

Wendy threw the phone down and ran to the photo by her bed. She took a good look at the photo of her and her beautiful girls. It was a photo she'd looked at hundreds of times.

To her horror, she noticed that the picture frame was cracked. Who would do such a thing? She then noticed that the picture had been altered. Her daughters' faces were faded. She looked intently at it and noticed that she was wearing something different from the old photo. She was startled to see something in the background. It was the three of them in a gazebo, and behind them, where at one time there was nothing but trees and fence, there was a figure of a man. His face was too far back to identify. Wendy knew that there had been no one else in the backyard the day that the picture was taken, other than the three of them. She took a deep breath and started to panic. She dropped the frame, shattering the glass completely on the wooden floor. She grabbed the phone.

"You better keep your distance! I don't know who you are, but if you step one foot into this place again, I'll call the police!"

"You better watch it, Wendy. If you keep talking like that, I'm gonna hurt your daughters!"

"What, what do you mean?"

"I'm watching you...." The phone went dead. Wendy froze and dropped it on the floor. Fear ran through her body and she started to cry hysterically. She paced around the room and then fainted, hitting her head hard on the floor. Everything went black.

Recovering from her fall, not knowing how long she had lain there unconscious, she scrambled to her feet, threw some water on her face and looked into the mirror. What happened? Then it hit her. She dashed for the kitchen and searched frantically for her keys and jumped into her car.

Driving downtown, Wendy couldn't focus, her car swerving left and right over the rain-covered pavement. All she could think of were her two daughters, and the madman who threatened to harm them. Fear and anxiety filled her mind, as she passed many different stores along Beach Boulevard. She continued to look along the sidewalks and constantly searched her rear-view mirror, as if she were being watched at that moment.

"I'm watching you" was repeating over and over in her mind, as she did her best to drive straight. She had to move quickly. Her daughters' lives were in jeopardy. Had the maniac found them already? Would they still be alive when she found them?

Looking along the street, Wendy's eyes wandered, carefully searching for the Winners Outlet store. Her older daughter, Natasha, was manager of the always-crowded clothing store. She was afraid that the mysterious caller would have tried to attack her first, because her younger daughter was at school in class, surrounded by her peers. Safe, she thought. But was she really? It sounded like the madman had no limitations. It was as though he'd stop at nothing. To think of this made her nervous and scared; she felt like throwing up. It was turning into her worst nightmare … would she get to her daughters in time?

She pulled into the Winners parking lot and ran inside. She couldn't see her daughter from the front of the store. Maybe she was at the back in the manager's lounge. Is she hurt? Or worse, is she dead? This thought kept going over and over in her mind, as she raced to the back of the store. She got to the lounge and pushed the door open in a panic. Her daughter was sitting in the corner of the room, holding her face and crying profusely.

"Are you hurt? What's wrong? What did he do to you and did you see who did it?"

Natasha looked up and saw her mother in distress.

"He hurt me, mom! I'm scared! I think he broke my nose … whoever he was."

"You didn't see the guy?" Wendy asked.

"NO! He snuck up from behind me!"

"Where were you?"

"I was in here! I was by myself. I came in to get a coffee and read the paper. I was sipping my coffee and someone came up behind me and hit me on the head. I turned and screamed and he hit me again, in the face. Blood was trickling and it hurt to push on my nose. I then tried to turn around to see who it was. I couldn't tell because he was a wearing a mask and my eyes were blurry. Then he ran out."

"We gotta get out of here!"

MEANWHILE …

It was 10:15 am. Paris sat in her classroom staring at the clock. The teacher was reading a novel to the class. All of a sudden, there was a ruckus in the hallway.

"What was that?" the teacher exclaimed. She walked into the hall and noticed all the other teachers peering out of their rooms. They were all surprised to see a man in a mask coming quickly down the hall. He started shouting very loudly and told the teachers to get the hell out of the school.

"If you don't want anyone hurt, listen to me right now! BACK OFF!" The mysterious man pulled out a gun and flashed it at all the teachers in the hall. The doorways to the classrooms were packed with curious students, all trying to see what the commotion was about. Panic filled the classrooms when the word "gun" was yelled out by a grade 6 kid. Kids all over started to scream.

The man flashed a picture to the closest teacher.

"Have you seen this girl?"

"NO, never before," the teacher lied, as she glanced over to the grade 5 classroom teacher. It was a hint and a nod that the man noticed. He hurried over to the grade 5 class and searched the room for Paris. He shot a bullet into the air. The teacher screamed. All the kids ran for shelter, and many fell to the floor covering their faces. He grabbed the teacher, "Give me the girl! NOW! If I don't get her, just know that she is worth three others! You comply, we have no problems."

"Look!" The teacher pointed at the outside window to distract the attacker. The man quickly ran to the large window, giving just enough time for Paris to dart out the classroom door and down the hallway. He turned and caught a last glimpse of Paris exiting the doorway.

He pushed two kids out of the way and ran down the hall. Meanwhile, Paris, as a frightened child would, searched for the principal or custodian, someone that could protect her from this madman. Running toward the office, she noticed another gun on the floor. A police officer and a kid were lying there.

"Oh my God!" There was blood everywhere! There were people gathered around in shock. The boy was a grade 9 kid, a boy she knew from the high school. Was the policeman dead? Someone was checking his vitals.

"What happened? Oh, God! Everybody, clear out! He's coming!"

Everyone started to panic and push and shove. Paris turned to see the man running toward her. Another police officer veered around the corner of the hallway and stopped the man from reaching her. He was shot, but the delay was enough to allow her to get out of the school.

In front of the school, she heard her name being called. "PARIS!" It was Wendy.

"Mom, there's a man after me! He's got a gun!"

"Quick, honey! Get in the car and stay low!"

As the car pulled out of the parking lot, the man spotted it wheeling out onto the street. A bang came from the doorway, as the girls ducked and hid. The car swerved from side-to-side and they noticed the man heading toward another vehicle.

Wendy pulled a right onto the next street. She continued to look back in her rear-view mirror. They stayed on the main street for a while and decided that the highway would be a better escape for them. They might be able to shake the killer who was tracking them down.

"Stay low, stay calm, and stay quiet. Especially you, Paris!" She was starting to panic in the back seat.

They pulled onto the highway and moved into the busy lane. Hoping that they had lost him, Wendy looked into her mirror. Like a horror movie, there he was, right behind them. The killer tried everything to catch up to the car, but Wendy was moving too fast. Suddenly, the car phone rang.

"Who would be calling at this time? I don't need this! Hello?"

There was heavy breathing. "Look out. I'm coming!"

"What do you want? Who are you?"

Wendy didn't know what to do. Who was this man? What was going on? As she continued to watch him in the mirror, she had to make a quick decision.

"That's it mister, I'm calling the police right now!"

"What if I am the police?"

She was stunned. "Alright. We'll meet at my place, just you and me. There you can tell me what you want!"

In her rear-view mirror, she noticed the man slow down and exit the highway. Wendy decided to pull off at the next exit. She dropped her girls off at their grandmother's place where they stayed. She did this casually, trying not to look suspicious. She left the area to devise some type of plan, and headed back to her mother's place. Suddenly, it came to her. She knew who it was.

The girls got back into the car and off they went. There was no way she would be going back to her cabin tonight.

"That man is not a police officer. I am sure."

"Where are we going, mom?"

"To the lake…."

At the lake, Wendy and the girls got into a boat and started the motor. Everyone took their seats. After a few minutes on the water, the boat suddenly cut out and a leak began.

"What's happening?" Paris yelled. "Mom, there's a leak!"

The boat was quickly filling up with water and was starting to tip.

"It's gonna tip!"

The boat capsized as the three of them were pushed under water from the weight of it. All three heads popped up underneath in an air pocket.

"Mom, what happened?"

"Girls, listen up. I've got to tell you something. I made the boat overturn on purpose. That man from the school. He's after me. He's a man I knew from a long time ago. He's trying kill me. It's a long story. I owe him money and I don't have it right now. When your father was sick and unable to work, I borrowed money, a lot, from this man, to pay for the hospital bills, medications, and surgery. I always planned to pay him back, but I had to support you guys. He did not understand this, and ever since, I have received random death threats, letters, and phone calls. Apparently, he has found us. I don't know how because I've covered my tracks all these years."

"Why didn't you tell us about this?"

"I didn't want to frighten you. I had gone this far in keeping you safe, but that ended today."

"What are we going to do?"

"Here's the plan," Wendy said, reassuring them that things were going to be okay. "It is so important that he thinks I'm dead. We must make him think that I am no longer around. I will need full cooperation from you."

Alarmed, Paris spoke up, "But, mom, if you play dead, we'll never see you again!"

"Honey, I will write you secret letters to update you on what's happening in my life. Natasha, I am counting on you to support your sister and keep her safe."

"So, what's the plan, mom?" Natasha asked curiously.

"I'm going to New York City. I'm starting a business of my own under another name. My new name will be Laurel McBean. I am part owner of a catering business called Sea Food Catering. I will get the new phone number to you some way. Remember, I am no longer Wendy, even to you. This name can never be said again."

"Why? Why does this have to happen?" Paris asked, scared, upset and worried.

"Honey, it has to. It just has to. You have to keep my former life under wraps. Speaking about me will only cause trouble. Here's the story so that we are all on the same page. We were all out in the boat and the boat capsized causing us to fall into the water. Only you two survived. I went missing. Both of you were frantic. I was never found."

Natasha spoke up, "What's going to happen with us? When will you return? Will you ever return?"

"Someday, but not right now. Not until he is arrested and taken into custody. That's what I will be working on from afar."

"Where does he come from?"

"I wish I could tell you, but I can't right now. Speaking his name would jeopardize your lives … our lives. It has to be this way for now. Be strong for your sister, Natasha. Someone will be coming to your rescue shortly."

Wendy took a deep breath, gave a wink to her daughters and went under water. Being a former synchronized swimmer, she could hold her breath for a long, long time, without coming up for air. She approached an island that was a distance from the boat, and spotted Frank who helped her to shore. They entered his cabin, which was nearby. He would be part of her plan.

"Frank, I need help immediately! Remember this morning? It's a long story, but our lives are in danger."

"I do, Wendy. What can I do to help you right now?"

"My two daughters are under the capsized boat over there. I need you to protect them and get them out of danger. I've pretended to have drowned. It is essential they both find shelter. I need you to take my girls safely to shore. You will meet a woman who is a close friend of mine. She is a part of the plan and she will be taking them from there. I will be flying out of Lake Louisiana, and the only people who will know where I am, and how I can be contacted are you, her, and my girls."

MEANWHILE …

"Natasha, I'm scared. What are we going to do?"

"We'll wait out here for a few more minutes until someone comes and helps us. Don't worry, mom will be safe."

In only moments, bubbles appeared around them. Frank had arrived.

He told the girls about the plan and what he was going to do. He said they'd be safe with him and that he was someone they could trust. He reiterated the plan. Before word got around about the accident, they followed Frank back to the sandy shore from which they set off, and were told to act shocked and pretend they knew nothing. Paris was told to pretend she had amnesia from a blow to the head. People began to gather on the sandy beach, many pointing out the boat in the water. They noticed three people approaching the shore.

"LOOK!" one man exclaimed.

The three of them exited the water, Frank with his arms around both girls. Natasha started to cry in panic.

"I don't know where my mom is. Or what happened to her. Can you help us?"

A lady stepped forward. Her name was Ginelle. "Honey, it will be fine."

The girls were brought to the ambulance. The police started to question the oldest about what had happened. How? Why? When? Natasha continued to tell the police her side of the story. Then, as directed by

Frank, the girls went with Ginelle. She told police she was a close friend of their mother's and that she would protect and take care of them. Frank stayed for questioning. The girls were very good at acting their parts, but were confused and upset, wondering if their mom would be safe. Ginelle took them home with her. The girls left the beach crying and in disarray. All part of the plan.

"JC Lincoln, reporting live from Harbour Bay in Lake Louisiana. At approximately 1:30 pm, today, a boat capsized a half-mile from shore. One woman went missing, and her two daughters were found safely underneath the boat. They were brought to shore by a nearby swimmer. The girls were both unharmed; however, the younger girl is experiencing bouts of amnesia. The older daughter is still in shock. The whereabouts of their mother is still a mystery as police comb the water near this quiet harbour town on the shore of Lake Louisiana. The victim is 45-year-old Wendy Redfield. They are still trying to figure out what caused the accident. We ask that anyone who may have information, please report it to the Louisiana Police Department. Your information will remain confidential. This is JC Lincoln, reporting live from Harbour Bay in Lake Louisiana."

Ginelle drove down the highway, heading toward her home. The two girls sat in the back, staring out the window, watching the cars pass by. Ginelle was worried. Really worried.

"Girls, listen up. I want to assure you, your mom will be fine. She is safe. You are aware of the man who has been stalking you and your mother. He seems determined to find and hurt your mother. We are still trying to find out things. For now, all you know is that your mother has died in the accident and you are both distraught and devastated. We must be on a continual lookout for this man. You will stay with me for now. I don't know when your mother plans to return, but she is flying to New York City this evening. Remember, you know nothing about this. We must keep these facts hidden, or all our lives will be in jeopardy. Stay hushed. Keep quiet. This is not over and we are not sure what the stalker has planned next."

"Can we contact mom?"

"Not right now. Not yet. We're hoping that he will give up if he thinks your mom is dead."

She drove into the city and headed toward her apartment. It would be the safest place to stay.

WEDNESDAY, 9:30 pm …

That evening, at the airport, Wendy boarded and left for New York under her new name. She had warned her daughters not to say anything that would cause suspicion. She had also told them not to worry, but to avoid calling her number unless it was an emergency. She'd said that if she heard it ring, she'd know it was them. No one else had the number. She would secretly return once the dust settled.

The plane flew off without Wendy ever noticing that she was being followed. She would soon find out that they were in a bigger mess than she had anticipated. Their lives were in turmoil already; however, things were about to get worse.

ONE WEEK LATER …

The girls were staying at Ginelle's place. It was on a Wednesday morning at 8:00 that they received the call.

"Hello?" Natasha answered.

"Do you know who this is?"

Natasha replied, "No, of course not!"

"I'll give you three guesses. The first two don't count."

"Oh, yah, sure!"

The man then shouted, "Do you think this is a joke?"

"I don't know. Who is this? Is that you, Steve? You're scaring me."

"NO, this is not Steve!"

"Well then, who is this?" she asked cautiously.

"I know where your mother is."

Natasha gulped and dropped the phone. It was him! It was the man who had been after them. He had found them! She stared at the phone lying on the floor, wondering whether to pick it up again or just get help. She picked up the phone again. This was the call they had feared.

"What do you want? What are you after? What did we do to you?"

"You ran away from me once! It won't happen again!"

"LEAVE US ALONE!"

"I know your mother's alive, and you will lead me to her!"

"What do you mean? My mom is dead!"

"Stop your lying! I know she's alive."

"Well, where is she?"

"In New York City."

"How do you know?"

"I have my sources. Besides, I'm not going to find her. She's going to find me!"

"What do you mean?" Natasha asked confused.

"I'll show you what I mean RIGHT NOW!"

Suddenly, a door slammed downstairs. Natasha ran into her sister's room and grabbed her arm, throwing her cell phone to the floor.

"He's here! He's here!"

"Who's here?"

"The guy is here! The guy that's after mom! He's after us! We gotta get Ginelle! She's in her room!"

They shuffled down the hallway and barged into Ginelle's room. To their surprise, the man was standing next to Ginelle, who had been knocked out, and was lying unconscious on her bed.

"Oh my God!"

The man reached for the girls. First, he grabbed Paris and pulled her toward the bed. Ginelle was bound at the wrists and the ankles. Natasha screamed, "What are you doing? LEAVE HER ALONE!" She pulled his arm. It startled him and he began to wrestle with them. It became a war, a battle of who wanted it more. Suddenly, Paris broke free and ran to the window. She opened it up and started yelling for help. The man wrestled her to the floor. Natasha leapt at him hoping to knock him over. She jumped onto him, hitting him in the head, hoping this would knock him out. Instead, an elbow came from out of nowhere, knocking Natasha down.

"What are you doing? Get away from her!"

The man grabbed a scarf and tied Paris' arms together. He dragged her into his car as Natasha arrived at the doorway. She was too late.

"NATASHA, HELP!"

"Tell your mother to meet me at the mall, 3rd floor, alone. 7 PM sharp! I'll be the one with the frantic kid!"

AT THE MALL THAT NIGHT …

They entered the 3rd floor clothing store. It was the perfect place to hide.

"Hi. I'd like to buy a blouse for my daughter." He looked toward Paris, trying to look like a normal father and daughter. He had removed the scarf from her wrists.

150

Paris wanted to run away, or yell out, but a gun was being held to her back. She was helpless.

Oblivious to the present danger, Sue, the store clerk replied, "I'll be right back. What colour are you looking for? What size? What pattern?"

He was getting irritated with all the questions Sue was asking.

"OH, NEVER mind! Whatever, whatever!"

Paris stood there silently, panic on her face.

"JUST GET IT!" he roared frantically with anger.

Sue made her way into the back room. Another woman entered the store. The man made a quick adjustment so that the gun could not be seen.

"Hi. How are you?"

"I'm ok," he said with frustration.

"That's good."

Suddenly, through the store window, the stalker noticed a man in uniform.

"Oh, God," he gasped.

The two of them weaved in behind the clothing racks, among the large winter coats. Trying to hide, he stuffed a scarf into her mouth.

"Hmmmh … hmmmh."

He threw her down onto the ground. All of a sudden, the two of them noticed the woman who had spoken to them at the cash. She was approaching, looking at other apparel.

The two of them were practically crawling on the floor, the stalker hoping the lady would just get the heck out!

"Your mother is too damn late! If I can't kill your mother, I'll kill you!"

The woman noticed Paris and the man on the floor.

"WHAT ARE YOU DOING?" the woman yelled.

"GET OUT OF HERE! IF YOU DON'T LEAVE, THIS GIRL DIES!"

The woman courageously jumped on him. The gun flew into the air and landed in Paris' hand. She fumbled with the gun and threw it to the lady. The lady pointed the gun at him and said, "Leave her alone!"

With a swift kick, the man hit the woman and she fell to the floor. The gun slipped out of her hand. The stalker reached for it.

"Now it's time for me to kill you both. I don't know who you are, lady, but this isn't your lucky day. You got in the way and now you're going to pay!"

At that exact moment, all the clothing racks around the three of them fell to the floor. Police officers pointed their guns at the man.

"You're under arrest! Drop the gun!"

"How did you find us?" the man asked, confused. He threw the gun down.

"That lady led us to you."

A mask was peeled off and a wig fell to the ground. Shocked, Paris stared into the woman's eyes.

"MOM!" She hugged her tightly. "What are you doing here? I thought you were in New York!"

"I was. I was hiding out for a while and thinking of a way to get this guy arrested or put in jail. He's been tracking you since our boat "accident" at the beach. He's no longer going to hurt us, any of us. They now know the truth. Come here, honey."

The two of them hugged for awhile, and went to the police station for questioning. They left at 9:00 pm. The family was finally free, and they were eager to go see Natasha and Ginelle and tell them what had happened. Wendy and Paris arrived at Ginelle's house. They found the two girls in a panic.

"MOM! Where'd you come from? What happened? Paris?"

"Everything has been taken care of. The man was arrested. He tried to kill us both, but we survived, with a lot of help from these." Wendy lifted up the mask and the wig, and breathed a sigh of relief. She gave Ginelle a hug.

With evening now upon them, they sat in the kitchen, sipping tea and talking about the craziness of everything. It was really unbelievable.

RRRRRING, RRRRRING …

Wendy got up and walked over to her cell phone.
"Hello?"
She heard heavy breathing on the other end.
"Hello?"
She heard heavier breathing.
"Who is this?"
A deep voice spoke out, "Do you lock your door at night?"
The line suddenly disconnected. Wendy hurried to the front door to ensure that it was locked.
"Mom, what's wrong? Who was that?"
Wendy looked at them.
"Um … it was nothing. Just a wrong number."
Wendy looked up at the kitchen clock.

Tick-tick-tick …

PART V

LOVE AND FAITH

"Love begins at home, and it is not how much we do ... but how much love we put in that action."

Mother Teresa

HE ENLIGHTENS ME
May 2014

Karen Lemieux

In my daily walk with Him,
He enlightens me through paths of righteousness for
His name's sake.
He is my supply and my need.
He leads me in the straight and narrow way.
I love Him so,
For He is so good to me.
Jesus, You put a song in my heart,
And the melody is ringing inside of me.
Your Holy Spirit enlightens me as well.
His gifts are many and His fruits abound.
It is a pleasure to know God is my Father.
Through Jesus, I will have eternal life.

WE'LL MISS YOU, JIM
November 2014

Judy Evans

A resident here, 2nd floor, at ROP,
Passed away, 5 am in his sleep.
I saw Hulse and Playfair take him in the elevator.
When alive, he was rude to me. I forgive, I forget.
Hope he went to Heaven. My sympathies, my
condolences to his family.
Hope he is at peace now.
In spite of everything, he was a good man.
Glad he was able to speak to his family.
On the phone, he smiled, was happy.
Hope he is having pleasant dreams.
He was content when he passed away.
Glad he was loved when he was alive.

GOD IS LOVE
February 2012

Sue Racine

God is love,
God is trust,
God is in my heart.

God is like the light
That shines,
In the morning
And the night.

God's arms cradle me
Unconditionally.
God is peace
And tranquillity.
God is the rock
Of my heart's desire.
God's arms cradle me
Unconditionally.

BRITTANY
June 2008

Judy Evans

Brittany is an awesome nurse,
Well trained, who works at ROP.
Conscientious, careful, excellent.
Never gets her medications mixed up.
Is good to us residents at ROP.
Loves her family.
Goes home to them.
Comes back next a.m. to the building.
Like all the other caregivers and nurses,
Works hard, earns her pay.
Goes home, comes back.
I like her, I like all the nurses.
They spoil us. Treat us well.
We are all safe here.
Our families come and visit us.
Brittany, long may you live, and work here.

JOHN'S WORDS TO LIVE BY
November 2011

John Cowie
(1938 – 2012)

"Righteousness exalteth a nation: but sin is a reproach to any people." Proverbs 14:34 KJV

DEFINITION: Morally correct behaviour ennobles a nation, but sin dishonours any people in any nation.

"Wisdom is before him that hath understanding; but the eyes of a fool are in the ends of the earth." Proverbs 17:24 KJV

DEFINITION: The ends of the earth are coal, oil, and gas. With understanding, one becomes wise in his ways.

Chris Nihmey

FAITH UNTOLD
October 2013

Karen Lemieux

Thou wilt my God I consent
To love Thee more, trust You more.
You lose it, if you don't have it. Hope.
The will to go on—to have more hope.

Without hope, you can't go on.
I put my faith in Thee,
Because of what He did for me,
On Calvary cross, of salvation for me.

He saved me from death and hell,
To look back no more
To my sins once before.
I am forgiven forever.

Forever the victory to the cross.
I will see Him once again someday.
In Heaven, a new paradise on earth,
A place for all to be together, You and me.
Without love, we are nothing.

LOVE
March 2010

Sue Racine

Love is like a river
That flows like
An unpredictable wind.
That moves at many levels
With layers of blues
And the deepest of reds.
That bleeds
Through the crystal-clear depths
Where my love and I
Share our secrets,
Until dawn do us part.

"Three things will last forever—faith, hope, and love—and the greatest of these is love."

1 Corinthians 13:13
Holy Bible
New Living Translation

IN MEMORIAM

FLY AWAY
January 11, 2011

Chris Nihmey for Nathalie Robillard

Since Nathalie could not verbalize her story, I wrote this to express her message of courage, strength, and hope.

This is a short story of an angel who came into my life. Her name is Nathalie.

For the last year and a half, I have volunteered helping Nathalie, and she has most definitely been my inspiration. Nathalie suffered from Huntington's disease, a terrible hereditary disease that took over every muscle of her body, including the ones in her face and tongue, disabling her speech. It caused her whole body to shake uncontrollably, even more than someone suffering from Parkinson's disease. Along with this, year after year, her brain also experienced a mental decline of its functions. The disease began in her early 20's and, by her 30's, Nathalie was bedridden, unable to walk or talk due to the severity of the disease. I first met Nathalie when she was 32, a year and a half ago, while volunteering at the residence where she lives, along with many others who suffer from physical and mental illnesses. Early on, I developed a genuine fondness for her, because of the beautiful person she was and the strength that she had but also, I have to admit, because of the reality of the life she lived, a life where she was alone … she was all alone. At the young age of 32, Nathalie had few friends and family, and was surrounded mainly by fellow residents, volunteers and workers who helped her at the home.

Over many months, I spent much time with Nathalie, going for walks, helping her with communication, sharing special times together, watching her favourite cartoons on TV, and spending time with her during meals. Although she could never share her words of appreciation with me, I always knew she cherished our times together. We both did.

Just after Christmas, Nathalie's health took a turn for the worse. She had to leave the home due to a virus that had entered her body, causing her core temperature to rise dramatically. That, on top of the disease, hurt her deeply. She went into emergency immediately and was admitted into the hospital for treatment. I found out a week later on my visit to the home. I was very surprised when I entered her room that day and she wasn't there. An empty space grew inside of me. I missed her instantly.

Not long after she left the residence, I decided I would pop in and visit Nathalie in the hospital. I took a stuffed dog from her room and planned to go some time the next week. I was driving home from the grocery store on the Friday night. It was January 7th, around 6:15, and for some reason, and I still can't understand why, I felt the need to turn the car around and go to the hospital that night. I didn't think much of it at the time, but it just felt like the right thing to do.

I took the elevator to the fifth floor and entered her room. There she was, sleeping like a baby on her stomach, head turned to the side. "Nathalie," I whispered. "Nathalie." She slowly opened her eyes and looked up at me. "Hi Nathalie ... it's Chris!" She quickly tried to turn onto her back to look at me. It always took a while for her to do this, but it was good to let her do it by herself, to build her strength. In a short time, she was looking at me and answering questions in short small breaths, more like grunts, as her muscles contracted quickly, and she actually ended up kicking me in the face! I laughed. She appeared to also. It was so great to see her and we spent a couple of hours together.

Early on, I placed her stuffed doggy on her stomach. She was very happy. Then I took out a little gift I had purchased from the gift shop … the perfect gift. It was a *Willow Tree* carving of an angel with wings holding a small butterfly, and it was perfectly named "Angel of Freedom". I went on to tell Nathalie that she would always be watched by God and His angel of freedom. And that someday soon, she would be free and, like a butterfly, would emerge from the cocoon she'd been imprisoned in for so long. My mother, reflecting on all I had been through, called me her elusive butterfly. Nathalie was mine. She would fly to a life free of pain, suffering, and hardship. I don't know what she understood from my words that night, it was hard to tell, but I do know she was listening and comforted as I spoke, as was I. I hope she understood. I like to think that she did.

That evening, we cherished our time together and I bade her farewell with a kiss on the cheek and a prayer. My kiss was so rare to her; little did I know that night how important that kiss would be.

Driving home, a lot of things about life came into perspective. What did it all matter? My house? My car? The things I owned? The reality was, none of it did matter. What mattered was the companionship and friendship that Nathalie and I had with each other. Wasn't that true of all things in life? It's really not all the things you "think you have", but more so the people "whom you have" in your life. Nathalie did not have much, but she had me, my friendship, my love and, most importantly, my prayers.

Three days following my visit with Nathalie, I received an upsetting phone call from the residence. On January 10, 2011, Nathalie had passed away. The pain, the discomfort, the heartache … it was over. It was a sad call; it was a happy call. She was out of the dark, and she was free. Nathalie was finally free! She was now with God, and she had emerged into a life free of the very things she'd been enslaved by. She would spread her wings and fly forever. For once, after a long time, she would feel warmth, happiness, and unending love.

I smile when I think about Nathalie flying off to her new home. I always thought that she was my angel, my angel of freedom, my inspiration for never giving up. But I guess, too, I was her angel on earth. Like she was an angel for me, I was one for her. I guess that's why our bond was so special, and why my final kiss to her that night was so precious, her last kiss, or maybe her first of many, depending on what side you look at things. I tend to think the latter.

I now dream of Nathalie running and jumping and playing like a child. I picture a smile on her face, and words coming out of her mouth, being able to eat on her own, and roll over in an instant. Boy, do I miss her already, but I know that my need to see her means little, because she is now free. Although I'll miss her dearly, I know most certainly that I will join her one day, and we will take a walk arm in arm. This time, however, we'll leave her wheelchair behind. Actually, it won't even be there!

God bless you, Nathalie. You're one of a kind. I can't wait to see you again. Until then, enjoy the life you should have always had. Embrace your new life. You deserve it, kiddo. Miss you ... dearly. Love Chris

Excerpt from *Two Sides To The Story: Living A Lie* by Chris Nihmey

Note: In the original version, the name "Nadia" was used for Nathalie to give her anonymity.

MAKING A DIFFERENCE

IF YOU AREN'T MAKING A DIFFERENCE, WHAT ARE YOU DOING?

"Be the change you want to see in the world."

Mahatma Gandhi

SPILL IT ALL OUT!

Chris Nihmey

Writing an anthology takes a lot of hard work and diligence. This was not an easy feat, but the rewards are endless. If you are interested in trying this out with your residents, students, or organizations, I highly recommend it. This was one of the greatest projects I've ever worked on. As an author, a fan of writing, I cannot express enough how fulfilling this project has been, and it all started with a simple question, "Tell me, what are you thinking about?" From there, the magic began. We need to be able to express our feelings, our emotions, in positive, life-building ways.

Following are two charts I composed. I began with these to open up each writer's mind. It is amazing what the mind can conjure. And sickness? It cannot stand in the way. It can only enhance creativity, helping draw out the mastery within. Oh, to be so beautiful....

I encourage you to try a project like this with your residents, students, or colleagues. Writing saved my life. It is therapeutic. It is amazing how powerful our thoughts can be, and when they are positively channelled, the possibilities are endless. The right support, compassion, and acceptance bring out the best in all of us, regardless of what we suffer from. From an idea, I took all writers through the whole process of writing, all the way to a finished product ready for publishing. It is astounding what can be accomplished.

"Think left and think right and think low and think high. Oh, the thinks you can think up if only you try!"

Dr. Seuss

WHAT'S ON YOUR MIND?

Think of an idea or a topic that might be of interest to you. Maybe animals, sports, friends, family, the circus, or even ice cream! It can be ANYTHING you want! Now **BRAINSTORM** everything you can about your topic.

PLAN YOUR STORY
WHAT WILL YOUR STORY BE?

Setting(s)	Characters

Plot

Themes	Problem(s)	Solution(s)

CONCLUSION

Chris Nihmey

We have been battered by sickness. We have experienced the worst, but have continued on. Mental illness has no favourites. It can hit anyone, at any time. We deserve to be respected and accepted. We contribute much to society and, with the right support surrounding us, healing has been possible and great things have happened. Remember that a step back is part of the process. It is not a reason to quit and give up. Trips and falls only make us stronger. They prepare us for a giant step forward the next time.

It all comes down to six prominent, powerful words. Our youth, our society as a whole is **"hurting"**. We are all hurting in some way, either personally, or for a loved one. When we hurt, we need to reach for **"help"**; with help comes **"hope"**. With hope comes **"healing"** and, ultimately, **"happiness"**. With healing comes the confidence and the assurance needed to succeed and make a difference. We are the key to our healing. We must grasp the reins of our own lives, and want to heal. Not only do we need to trust others, we must be able to trust and believe in ourselves, and know that we "can" improve: that healing is possible. Then, and only then, can we thrive.

However, none of this happens without the final **"H"**. It stands for **"heart"**. Without it, all is lost. If people do not open their hearts by listening, by accepting, by having compassion and empathy for someone who is suffering, who is reaching out, none of this happens. All hope is lost, and suffering continues. Not only is hope lost, the sufferer remains in isolation, and death is imminent. A supporter must open up their heart when someone reaches for help; otherwise, the person is ignored and the illness wins. A perfect example of this occurs every day, worldwide, country to country, city to city: society's negative perception and dehumanization of the homeless.

Daily, millions of people will "pass" by a sufferer, reaching a hand for some sort of help: money, food, friendship, or just an ear to listen. Some sort of hope. Without a hello, or even a simple smile or wave, we are already looking down at them with a judgemental and resounding "NO". Thus, acceptance, compassion, and hope fall to the wayside, and our fellow "neighbour" in need continues to struggle alone. It is not fair! No one ever chooses to live on the streets. Sickness, abuse, bullying, addiction, rejection, and isolation make this choice. The bottom line is this: without hope, we are nothing. Give someone even the smallest glimmer of hope, and the possibilities will flourish. That is the true power of hope. Without listening or acknowledging, we close the door to their healing. We all want love; we yearn for it. We want to feel self-worth. We need to know we are loved: to know that we matter.

Reflections From Another Side has a strong connection to my memoir **Two Sides To The Story: Living A Lie**. Where once I shared my side of the story, many survivors and advocates are now speaking up by writing and sharing their own stories. We each have a story to tell. There is always "another side" worth listening to.

Our illustrator, Mario Jamora, captures the true essence of hope. It is magnificent. Our front and back covers demonstrate the true power of providing hope. Hope is the butterfly that touches down in the water, sees its reflection, and leaves its imprint by creating ripples of positive change. As these ripples expand and spread wide, reaching further and further, much like the butterfly, our lives begin to change. One ripple at a time, one word at a time, one story at a time. Each writer is making a solid impact in the world of mental health and wellness, by educating, and creating awareness, thereby instilling change. This creates hope and healing in each of us. The whole pond (society) will then begin to change. Without **"heart"**, the ripples never form, and hope ceases to exist.

Transform your life and, like the butterfly, an image of incredible beauty, you will also help transform the lives of others. The butterfly, like us, represents hope, change, transformation, healing, and new life.

We come from every walk of life. Each of our journeys has been different, yet we each share one commonality. It is hope. It carries us and it sustains us. Without it, we are nothing. May you find hope in your journey and never, ever, let it go. You are not alone. Illness is not your fault. You matter in every way. Your fingerprint alone is a stamp of how unique you truly are. No one in this world shares the same print, or ever will. May you always stand united together with those who care to make a difference in your life. In turn, you will make a difference, in your life, and in the lives of others. All of us must face our own reflection, dig down deep within, and find our true selves, empowering us to be the people we should be. We have done this by sharing our stories. Share your life. Share your story. Who knows where your adventure will take you?

Never lose hope …

We have an illness. We are not the illness. See the person, not the illness.

Chris Nihmey

THANK YOU, MY FRIENDS

February 12, 2018

Dear Friends,

I have something I'd like to share with you. It is my way of showing my appreciation to all of you. I am very grateful and thankful for the things you have done, for not only me, but for all of us. It is gratitude for the wonderful things you do. You are not only my helpers, you are my true friends, and I fully appreciate the many things you do to make our home a home. A happy and safe place to live. Without your love and friendship, I, and so many others, would be depressed, would lose hope. You save us from that. You keep us standing tall. We feel wanted, cared for, respected, and loved.

Experiencing the difficulties I do, sometimes I feel that my thanks does not come across in the way I hope. It is much more than mere thanks. ROP has been a sanctuary for me and for all my fellow residents. It is not only a place where education and learning takes place, it is a home, where we enjoy many good times, but also many challenging times. More than anything, however, it is a place of healing. Despite the difficulties, I have to continue on. Everyone is trying to heal in their own way. You show patience, acceptance, compassion, and encouragement in all that you do. Each of you has taught me the value of not giving up. To not give up on myself, though the difficulties are many.

One word: challenging. Some days I just want to say "to heck with it". But I know if I do that, I'll become nothing, and all the work I've done will be wasted. A waste of time, a waste of energy, and a waste of hard work. All I've achieved would be for naught.

You, my friends, help me to keep moving forward and continue despite my setbacks. We've had some good days and some bad days but, overall, you've made my living here a very positive thing. We will continue to have ups and downs, but we know that things are going to be okay.

To my wonderful support and my incredible friends, in and out, far and wide ... thank you for making me feel special. It is what keeps me going on.

Thank you from deep within,

Love, Sue

"I won't cry, I won't cry, no I won't shed a tear, just as long as you stand, stand by me."

Stand By Me
Ben E King
Leiber & Stoller

June 17, 2017

Dear Diary,

A few days ago, I stumbled upon something. A book. A book that has really changed my perspective on things. I couldn't put it down! It is called **Reflections From Another Side**. It's amazing how your outlook can improve in one week. I have yet to finish reading it, but it has already given me hope, a reason to continue on. It's hard to believe that it happened. I have never believed that things just "happen for a reason". My mind wouldn't let me. I've lived in a shadow for too long. I see life a bit differently today. My life hasn't miraculously turned around. I still struggled to get up, I still didn't eat a normal breakfast, but something has changed today. For the first time in a long time, I see promise. I've taken a step forward. If these men and women can do it, so can I. It was a book with a message so profound. It told me that I CAN. It gave me hope. I never thought that I could find a way to fight my negative thoughts, and that they could be overcome.

Writing ... it changed their lives. You've got to read this thing! With a pen and paper, they found a trickle of hope, some purpose, some meaning in their lives, and it didn't stop there. A pen on paper reaches a few. Imagine what a whole book could do. Wow! Thus far, this book has taught me to share ... to share my agonies, to share my triumphs. Going through sickness, otherwise, is done in vain. I am going through this for a reason. I have to believe that, in time, there will also be a reason that I healed. If there was one underlying message this book carried, words of wisdom you might say, it was this; change is possible. Healing can happen. There is hope. I am not alone in my struggles. There are others out there walking a similar path. If they can, I can. We can. It is about acceptance and compassion. That's what they are fighting for. I will not stop the fight to gain the respect that I deserve.

I really believe that things are going to be okay now. I will not give up ... Anne

(see Introductory Journal)

RESIDENT WRITERS' BIOGRAPHIES

"Changing the world one person at a time."

Chris Nihmey

I AM PROUD TO INTRODUCE YOU TO THE ROP RESIDENT WRITERS

GREG BACON

Date of birth: May 23, 1959
Place of birth: England, UK
Education: grade 10
Previous Occupation: brief work in carpentry
Diagnosis: Diabetes, seizure disorder, mood disorder (uses wheelchair for mobility)
Likes: hockey, football

JOHN COWIE

June 20, 1938 – December 9, 2012
Place of birth: Port Perry, Ont.
Education: attended university (quarterback on football team)
Previous Occupations: construction, railroad worker
Diagnosis: Schizophrenia, Bipolar Affective Disorder, Chronic Kidney Disease, Osteoarthrosis

Likes: drama, poetry, the Holy Bible, and music

JUDITH EVANS

Date of birth: July 4, 1945
Place of birth: Toronto, Ont.
Education: 2 years of university in Art History and Drama
Previous Occupations: YMCA front desk, H&R Block receptionist, part-time worker at Toys "R" Us
Diagnosis: Schizophrenia and Depression
Likes: writing poetry, reading, painting

ELIZABETH GERVAIS

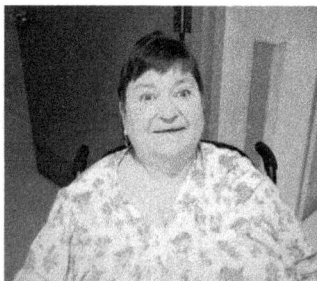

Date of birth: July 14, 1950
Place of birth: Pembroke, Ont.
Education: Teachers College (not completed)
Previous Occupation: hospital kitchen worker
Diagnosis: Schizophrenia (uses wheelchair for mobility)
Likes: all types of hats, playing solitaire

ELAINE GROOTHUYSEN

Date of birth: January 15, 1953
Place of birth: Ottawa, Ont.
Education: began university
(sickness destroyed this)
Previous Occupations:
food bank volunteer, night-
duty at a nursing home
Diagnosis: Paranoid
Schizophrenia
Likes: knitting, reading

LAILY KANT

Date of birth: January 30, 1966
Place of birth: New Delhi,
India
Education: Bachelor's
Degree in Sociology and
Spanish
Previous Occupation:
ESL teacher
Diagnosis:
Schizophrenia, Type 2
Diabetes
Likes: painting, writing, reading

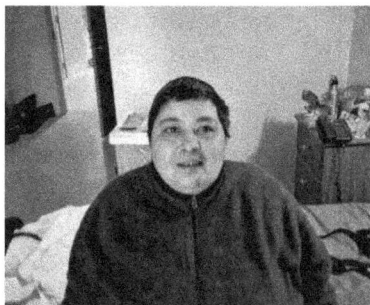

KAREN LEMIEUX

Date of birth: July 14, 1963
Place of birth: Cornwall, Ont.
Education: grade 11
Previous Occupations: work
experience in school
program, volunteer work
Diagnosis: Bipolar Affective
Disorder (uses wheelchair for
mobility)
Likes: her faith in Jesus,
dance, painting, writing

DAVID MALLETT

Date of birth: September 9, 1960
Place of birth: Ottawa, Ont.
Education: grade 12
Previous Occupations: Y's
Owl Co-op, government
work
Diagnosis: Anxiety
Disorder, Personality
Disorder, Depression,
Congestive Heart Failure
(CHF)
Likes: music, building a strong faith life

MICHAEL MARTIN

Date of birth: April 30, 1948
Place of birth: Unknown
Education: grade 10
Previous Occupations:
library worker, assembly
worker
Diagnosis: Paranoid
Schizophrenia, Asthma,
Dementia, Dysphasia &
Aphasia, Chronic Obstructive
Pulmonary Disease (COPD)
Likes: drawing, poetry, strong faith life

DANNY PARENT

Date of birth: October 30, 1947
Place of birth: Gatineau, Quebec
Education: grade 7
Previous Occupation:
worked at a lawyer's office
Diagnosis: Schizophrenia,
Personal History of Alcohol
Abuse, Homeless for 20 yrs.
Likes: Checkers, Chess,
Music (The Beatles),
Mars & Caramilk bars

DICKENS PIERRE-LOUIS

Date of birth: March 23, 1963
Place of birth: Haiti
Education: College
Previous Occupation:
Registered Nurse
Diagnosis: Focal Brain
Injury, Type 2 Diabetes
(uses wheelchair for
mobility)
Likes: Connect 4, cars,
music, movies

SUSAN RACINE

Date of birth: July 21, 1962
Place of birth: Ottawa, Ont.
Education: grade 12
Previous Occupations:
secretary for the government,
tutoring on speech
Diagnosis: Depression,
Anxiety Disorder, Dyskinetic
Cerebral Palsy, Glaucoma,
Chronic Pain (uses
wheelchair for mobility)
Likes: writing, reading, listening to reading,
dogs and cats

NATHALIE ROBILLARD

April 4, 1977 – January 10, 2011
Place of birth: Unknown
Education: Unknown
Previous Occupation: Unknown
Diagnosis: Huntington's disease
Likes: watching television, listening to a story, going for walks in her wheelchair

ROBILLARD, Nathalie (1977 – 2011) Died peacefully in hospital, on Monday, January 10, after a long, courageous struggle with Huntington's disease.

BEVERLEY SUNDAY

Date of birth: August 30, 1979
Place of birth: Edmonton, AB
Education: College (Business Management)
Previous Occupations: Fitness Instructor, Dancer
Diagnosis: brain injury, moderate visual impairment, hemiplegia of non-dominant side (uses wheelchair for mobility)
Likes: dancing, writing, strong faith life

RESOURCES

Speak up! There are always people to reach out to, people who will be there to listen, to guide, and to provide hope, so that you can begin to heal. Remember that with help comes hope, and with hope comes healing. Here are some organizations you can trust, to give you the help you need and point you in the right direction. Whether you are a sufferer, or a supporter, educating yourself is crucially important. We cannot fear. With understanding comes compassion and acceptance.

My website: www.chrisnihmey.com

My publisher: www.chipmunkapublishing.co.uk

In Ottawa:

Royal Ottawa Mental Health Centre
Ottawa: 613-722-6521 / Brockville: 613-345-1461
www.theroyal.ca

Mental Health Crisis Line – Ottawa: 613-722-6914
Toll-Free: 1-866-996-0991 – www.crisisline.ca

Kids Help Phone – Toll-Free: 1-800-668-6868
www.kidshelpphone.ca

Youth Services Bureau YSB: 613-729-1000
24/7 Crisis Line – Ottawa: 613-260-2360
Toll-Free: 1-877-377-7775 Mental Health Services:
613-562-3004 – www.ysb.ca

Distress Centre of Ottawa and Region – Ottawa:
613-238-3311 – www.dcottawa.on.ca

And beyond:

Canadian Alliance on Mental Illness and Mental Health – www.camimh.ca

Bell Let's Talk – https://letstalk.bell.ca/en/

Healthy Minds Canada www.healthymindscanada.ca

Canadian Psychiatric Association – www.cpa-apc.org

American Psychiatric Association – www.apa.org

Canadian Mental Health Association www.cmha.ca

National Institute of Mental Health www.nimh.nih.gov/index.shtml

National Alliance on Mental Illness – www.nami.org

Mind Your Mind – www.mindyourmind.ca

Rethink Mental Illness – www.rethink.org

SANE Mental Health Charity – www.sane.org.uk

MIND for Better Mental Health – www.mind.org.uk

Thank you, reader, for your interest and support.

"I'm only one, but still I am one. I cannot do everything, but still I can do something; and because I cannot do everything, I will not refuse to do something that I can do."

Helen Keller

AUTHOR BIOGRAPHY

Chris Nihmey is an Ottawa-based mental health advocate, author, presenter, and teacher. He was selected as a **2017-18 Ambassador for the Canadian Alliance on Mental Illness and Mental Health.** Please visit www.camimh.ca for more details on the campaign and their many partner organizations. As a **Face of Mental Illness** he was chosen to continue the fight to destroy the stigma of mental illness. Five faces are chosen each year to be Canadian Ambassadors for mental health and wellness. The organization's most prominent sponsor is Bell Let's Talk, Canada's largest campaign for mental health: *letstalk.bell.ca/en/* One of the focal points of both campaigns is to balance government funding evenly between mental and physical health in Canada. Ultimately, mental illness is a physical illness, dramatically affecting our brain, and causing pain.

Graduating from Western University in 1998, Chris had the world in his hands, his future fully planned. Sickness changed everything. After a diagnosis of Bipolar Disorder at 26, he was forced to end his teaching career abruptly. Two years later, he was additionally diagnosed with Obsessive-Compulsive Disorder and Generalized

Anxiety Disorder. Chris made a decision to hide his illnesses, keeping them a secret while resorting to supply teaching. Alongside faith, his doctor, numerous therapies, an incredible family and much support, medications, and much hard work, he made recovery a full-time job. In 2007, he began writing a story about his battle. This became a driving force in his healing, bringing him purpose and meaning. He now writes and speaks, to fight stigma, and to provide inspiration, hope, and healing. Chris has written and published several books, while continuing to promote awareness and change. He has spoken at well over 100 venues: schools, including universities and colleges, organizations, and the Ottawa Police Force.

His memoir, **Two Sides To The Story: Living A Lie**, describing his battle with mental illness, was released in 2013, a story giving hope to sufferers and their loved ones. In 2016, he released an illustrated picture book, **Sally**, a story which humanizes the homeless by giving them a voice. Chris combined forces with illustrator, Mario Jamora, whose breathtaking images added significantly to a life-changing story. **Reflections From Another Side: Mental Illness Survivors and Advocates Unite to Write**, is his latest publication in 2018. Two new books are currently being prepared for publishing. All these books are published by Chipmunka Publishing, in the UK. His books sell in Ottawa Chapters stores, and online globally at Indigo, Amazon, and Barnes & Noble, as well as other sites worldwide. Please visit **www.chrisnihmey.com** for more information on his books and initiatives.

Through writing and speaking, Chris aims to further educate and create awareness in hopes of eliminating the fear that prevents us from understanding mental illness and its effects on all of us. His message is one of hope. With hope … healing does happen.

ILLUSTRATOR – MARIO JAMORA

Mario Jamora is the illustrator of the picture book, Sally, a heartwarming story connecting mental illness and homelessness. His breathtaking illustrations combine together with an unforgettable story of giving and never losing hope in the midst of loss.

Mario earned a Bachelor's Degree of Fine Arts in Major-Commercial Design and Advertising, from the University of the Philippines. He took post grad studies in Illustration and Design under Milton Glaser at the School of Visual Arts in New York City, as well as Printmaking at Pratt Institute in Manhattan. He started his career in Consumer Advertising at McCann Erickson Intl., and Doyle Dane Bernbach NY. He then moved on as Art Director in Pharmaceutical Advertising at Sudler and Hennessey NY, eventually becoming VP Associate Creative Director at Lyons Lavey Nickel Swift, NY. Throughout his career, Mario has also worked on freelance illustration projects for McGraw-Hill Publishing, and Scholastics Magazines and Books. He garnered numerous awards from the RX Club of NY, the Society of Illustrators of NY, and the Art Directors Club of NY. Currently, Mario's passion is in Digital Photo Illustration and he is represented by the July Group Illustration Agency at **www.thejulygroup.com**